My friend, Kent Humphreys, has a unique entr̲...̲ ̲...̲ ̲...̲ ̲...̲ ̲...̲ ̲...̲ ̲...̲ ̲...̲ ̲...̲ ̲...̲ ̲...̲ need and then filling it in a way no one else has and he has done it again with this great book *In Your Transition*. Hopefully it will become to the college grad what Good to Great has become for every business leader…a must read and companion for success!

Dr. Mark Cress, Founder/President
Corporate Chaplains of America, Inc.

Kent Humphrey's newest book is practical and packed with wisdom birthed through experiences with God and work. The transition from school to the workplace is difficult. This book will help you get off to a great beginning. I wish I had such a resource when I graduated from college!

Randall Adams, Ph.D
Leader of the Church Outreach Team
Baptist General Convention of Oklahoma

It should be obvious by now that college does not always prepare students, particularly those interested in following Christ, for life outside of the university setting. Call it a 'quarter-life crisis' or whatever you'd like to, but the reality is that the sort of transitional help this book provides has been sorely needed for some time. Among its many strengths is its breadth - it covers many, many of the challenges that plague students during their transitional years. I will certainly encourage the many college students and campus ministers I work with to utilize this resource!

John Stonestreet
Executive Director
Summit Ministries

I am very excited about *Christ@Work, In Your Transition*. The danger of dualism is dealt with directly and clearly as well as the value of Kingdom-thinking and living. This book will be an invaluable resource to any recent grad!

Joe Maschhoff
20s Mission Director
Navigators

Kent Humphreys has compiled an encouraging book that highlights the providence of God for all young leaders moving into their life's occupation. Work in business is a high calling of God, with a sacred meaning and purpose as we move in His Kingdom vision. In addition to the transition of business to produce beneficial goods and services for a profit, eternal results can occur, as Kent and the authors note. These results are realized when God's children understand His calling on their lives, find their place of business and ministry in Him, and integrate into a community of peers, ideally with a mentor. As the next generation of leaders integrates their faith and work, to help along the journey, they become vital building blocks in the development of Christ's Kingdom, *as shared in Christ@Work, In Your Transition.* By following the precepts outlined by these authors, the essence of our humanity in Christ will bring eternal value; the people in our marketplaces become the subject of our labor, not just the object of our work, producing incredible personal fulfillment to those who transition into the marketplace in obedience to Christ.

Tom Phillips
VP of Festivals and Crusades
Billy Graham Evangelistic Association

Kent is a high energy gold mine of inspirational wisdom. I have filled 23 Passport pages the last 12 months, traveling with the purpose of building bridges between the marketplace and ministry. I have seen all over the world how Kent & his writings are valued, applied and distributed. This book will affirm, confirm & empower your calling as a marketplace minister.

Tom Webb
International Business as Missions (BAM) Advocate
Youth with a Mission (YWAM)

What Kent has written has been needed for years. It's so practical, so clear, yet challenging and empowering. The wisdom he and his fellow authors provide in these pages is priceless. This is what I have been looking for for years. I will definitely be using it with our students as well as our directors. It's a gem.

John Strappazon
Oklahoma State Campus Director
Director of Oklahoma Baptist Collegiate Ministries

Kent Humphreys and his team have done a great job showing young professionals how they can make a lasting impact for Christ in the marketplace. May the Lord powerfully use this book to influence the next generation of world-changers.

Dr. Bill Jones
President
Columbia International University

Christ@Work, *In Your Transition from the Campus to the Workplace* offers the advice and spiritual direction needed by this generation of college students. The wisdom and discernment in this book will guide many graduating college students into a closer walk with Christ and a more successful transition into the next stage of their lives.

Chris Goree
Campus Minister at The University of Oklahoma
InterVarsity Christian Fellowship

One of the great challenges we are facing in campus ministry is how to prepare our grads to transition from the campus into the workplace. *Christ@Work, In Your Transition from the Campus to the Workplace* Is a valuable resource which will give college graduates wisdom, encouragement, and hope as they seek to labor in the Kingdom. I wholeheartedly recommend this book to anyone seeking to transition well into the marketplace.

Jim Luebe
Collegiate Director
U.S. Navigators

Kent Humphreys has written a niche book. That's what makes it so powerful! You "qualify" for its distinctive message if you're committed to Christ and transitioning from college to the world of everyday work. Make it your indispensable companion. It will impact the rest of your life.

John D. Beckett
Chairman, The Beckett Companies
Author: *Loving Monday* and *Mastering Monday*

KENT   HUMPHREYS

CHRIST@WORK
IN YOUR
TRANSITION

FROM THE CAMPUS TO THE WORKPLACE

Published by
Lifestyle Impact Ministries
Kent Humphreys
PO Box 271054
Oklahoma City, OK 73137-1054
Phone: 405-949-0070 x102 or 405-917-1681 x102
Email: kent@fcci.org or khumphreys@ahpartners.com
Website: www.lifestyleimpact.com

Book design: C R Design, Charles Rogez, 405-550-9176

Some of the anecdotal illustrations in this book are true to life and are included with the permission of the persons involved. All other illustrations are composites of real situations, and any resemblance to people living or dead is coincidental.

Unless otherwise identified, all Scripture quotations in this publication are taken from the HOLY BIBLE: NEW AMERICAN STANDARD UPDATED® (NASU®). Copyright © 1973, 1978, 1984 by International Bible Society. Used by permission of Zondervan Publishing House. All rights reserved. Other versions used include: the New International Version (NIV), © The Lockman Foundation 1960, 1962, 1963, 1968, 1971, 1972, 1973, 1975, 1977; The New Testament in Modern English (PH), J. B. Phillips Translator, © J. B. Phillips 1958, 1960, 1972, used by permission of Macmillan Publishing Company; THE MESSAGE (MSG). Copyright © 1993, 1994, 1995, 1996, 2000, 2001, 2002. Used by permission of NavPress Publishing Group; The Living Bible (TLB), Copyright © 1971, used by permission of Tyndale House Publishers, Inc., Wheaton, IL 60189, all rights reserved; and the Good News Bible Today's English version (TEV), copyright © American Bible Society 1966, 1971, 1976.

Humphreys, Kent.
  Christ @ Work - In Your Transition. From the Campus to the Workplace
Includes bibliographical references.
  1. Evangelistic work. 2. Witness bearing (Christianity) 3.Work--Religious aspects--Christianity. I. Title.

ISBN: 978-0-9843575-2-9

DEDICATION

This book is dedicated to the thousands of campus ministers and Christian faculty on university campuses who daily give their lives to train the next generation of Christian leaders.

ACKNOWLEDGEMENTS

This project could have never been completed without the help of leaders from many campus ministries. Their servant hearts and kingdom attitudes have enabled me to put together a book that will be a resource of help to graduates for years to come. The following people have contributed chapters, gave counsel and input to the project, gave their patience to me, and freely provided their resources to the reader.

Bob Anderson *Christian Challenge*

Max Barnett *Seminary Professor of Collegiate Ministry*

Mike Blackwell *VP at Columbia International University*

Dave Edwards *Pastor of River Church*

Laurie & Chris Goree *InterVarsity Christian Fellowship*

Jon Kelsey *Baptist Collegiate Ministries*

Amy Kress *Hillsdale College Graduate*

Mark Lewis *The Navigators*

Christian Overman *Worldview Matters*

Chuck Price *Campus Crusade for Christ*

Dave Riner *Student Mobilization*

Craig Seibert *Priority Associates*

Jeremy Story *Campus Renewal Ministries*

Sarah Kirk *InterVarsity Christian Fellowship*

Bob Varney *Campus Crusade for Christ*

My heartfelt thanks is extended to all of you,

Kent Humphreys

FORWARD

For over 50 years I have ministered to university students. I have seen the difficulties and shock they face upon graduation and moving into the workplace.

They deal with a new schedule, location, work environment, associates, friends, church, living situation, and sometimes with a new marriage or parenthood responsibilities. Often those who showed such promise as Christians in the university are largely lost to the cause of Christ. They feel unprepared for the world they face. Many give up the spiritual aspirations they had in college and join the masses of ineffective believers.

Kent Humphreys made the transition from the university to the workplace successfully. For over 40 years in the workplace, he has learned many lessons he longs to share with you. I doubt you will ever find a book that will help you more in making a successful transition into the workplace. Read it carefully and often. It will be a faithful counselor through life. Share copies with others who also desperately need the counsel therein.

Max Barnett

CONTENTS

CONTENTS

INTRODUCTION

"As You sent Me into the world, <u>I also have sent them into the world...</u> I do not ask on behalf of these alone, but for those also who believe in Me through their word; that they may all be one; even as You, Father, are in Me and I in You, that they also may be in Us, so <u>that the world may believe</u> that You sent Me."

John 17:18-21

"<u>Go therefore and make disciples of all the nations,</u> baptizing them in the name of the Father and the Son and the Holy Spirit, teaching them to observe all that I commanded you; and lo, I am with you always, even to the end of the age."

Matthew 28:19-20

You are in a time of transition, and I want to be a real encouragement to you in this season of your life. While reading this book, you are going to receive hope, direction, and practical pointers which will enable you to successfully enter into the next exciting phase of your life with Christ. I am assuming three things about you as we begin our journey together:

1. That you are a committed <u>follower of Jesus Christ</u>. You may have been involved in a student ministry on a secular campus for a few years, or you may have been attending a Christian university and participated in many of the activities there. Or you may not have had the time to be involved in a student ministry or activities because of class schedules or working, but your walk with Christ is still very important to you.

2. That you are <u>still making the transition</u> to the workplace, whether you are in your last year on the campus, or you have left the campus during the last few months, or that you left several years ago and have yet to make the transition in several key areas of your life.

3. That you are not going into full-time vocational Christian service such as a campus student ministry, seminary, the pastorate, church staff, or missions. This booklet is not primarily for those students, but it is for the other 90%, the "non-professionals", who are entering the workplace and want to impact it for Jesus Christ.

Let me take you to the scriptures and the last evening that Jesus had with His friends just before the cross. (Go to Mark 14 or one of the other gospels.) It was graduation time. The events of the next couple of days would change them forever. Jesus had spent three years with the disciples, and now they would be severely tested. The twelve of them had the meal together, and then Judas left to begin his treachery. Jesus took the remaining eleven to the garden and asked them to sit and watch while He prayed. He took the three to be a little closer to Him. Then He fell on his face before the Father and prayed the prayer of John 17. When Jesus finished praying, He announced that the time had come, and within moments Judas and the soldiers arrived. The Scriptures say that within just a few minutes, *"... they all left Him and fled."* (Mark 14:50)

In Mark 14:70-72 we read, *"And after a little while the bystanders were again saying to Peter, "Surely you are one of them, for you are a Galilean too." But he began to curse and swear, "I do not know this man you are talking about!" Immediately a rooster crowed a second time. And Peter remembered how Jesus had made the remark to him, "Before a rooster crows twice, you will deny Me three times." And he began to weep."* Peter, who had always been the strong leader, and was the only one to hang around, was quick to deny his Lord. In this time of transition, you may be beginning to feel a little like Peter and the other disciples. Jesus had predicted the scattering in John 16:31-32, *"Do you now believe? Behold, an hour is coming, and has already come, for you to be scattered, each to his own home, and to leave Me alone;"* It may seem to you that everyone is going in a different direction, and that the close fellowship you have enjoyed the last few years has ended or is in the final process of being changed forever. Over a couple of years you have made the deepest friendships in your life, and now you are being scattered to various cities.

Even Paul had to deal with the loss of his closest friends. In 2 Timothy 4:16-17 Paul shares, *"At my first defense no one supported me, but all deserted me; may it not be counted against them. But the Lord stood with me and strengthened me."* There are seasons of life. In some seasons we gather and meet new friends, and in others we are scattered to different places and new situations. This is a season in which you will make some of the most important decisions of your life. You will be making choices concerning a possible life mate, your career, where you will live, and what key friendships you will establish. You will be choosing a specific type of church and Christian fellowship and will be establishing certain personal spiritual habits that will become life patterns. And you may be making those choices without the very close friends that you have made over the last few years.

You may be asking questions like these which are from students who are just beginning or currently in transition from the campus to the workplace:

- There are so many seemingly good options and opportunities, how can I know which one is <u>God's will</u> for me?

- What is God's <u>specific call</u> on my life? Can I have the same significance in the workplace as those who are going into vocational ministry?

- How much of a role should my feelings and the passions of my heart play in making a <u>career decision</u>?

- How do I find, get plugged into, and <u>cultivate community</u> in a new place where I do not know anyone?

- How do I start looking for the right <u>local church,</u> and how do I adapt to a totally different worship environment?

- What are some of the ways that I can <u>integrate my faith</u> and bring Jesus into a secular workplace?

- How can a find an older <u>mentor</u> who can guide me through those tough decisions?

- Is it possible to find my <u>passion</u> and fulfill my dreams while making a living?

- What are some types of <u>ministries</u> that I should get involved in once I graduate and enter the workplace?

- How do I get on a firm foundation <u>financially</u> and begin to learn more about credit, debt, budgets, investing, and the economy?

In the following brief chapters, we will share a few things in each of these areas in which you will be making choices. We will first address this whole issue of calling, and determine if you really are the "second class citizen" that you may feel like because you did not go on staff with a student ministry or off to seminary with some of your good friends from the Christian university. You have chosen to go into the secular workplace and represent Jesus Christ.

Secondly, we will give you some practical help as you seek to find that perfect job, great church, new group of friends, and possibly a life time partner. We will also share with you how you can find a wise mentor and your place of service in the Body of Christ. We will talk about the issues of "living intentionally among the lost" and not getting trapped in the religious community. Finally, we will deal with the practical issue of finances. We will share with you how you can finance your dreams and avoid the pitfalls as you navigate the swift currents in the financial rivers of life.

Continually, we will focus on the above two Scriptures from John 17 and Matthew 28. As you move out into this new world to which He has sent you, consider this question:

"In this time of your transition, how do you <u>obey</u> His command to make disciples and, in unity, also <u>represent</u> and glorify Him, in order that many may believe?"

Since I am over sixty years of age, I do not understand your world on the campus, your music, your technology, or how you think. Our guest authors in Section II do understand those things. However, I understand the workplace that you will be entering. I have spoken to student groups of various campus ministries over the last thirty years. I have addressed numerous MBA classes and business schools. It has been my privilege to have taken hundreds of students and young executives out to lunch and answer many of their questions about the workplace, business, and life. Not only have I spoken across our nation addressing the topic of the workplace, but in recent years I have traveled to over twenty nations helping business leaders integrate their faith and work. In Section I, I will be sharing some of the principles that others have found helpful as they have made successful transitions into the marketplace.

Chapters in Section II have been written by leaders from some of the key campus ministries, a pastor who ministered on campus for years and now pastors a church for these "transition grads", an executive of a Christian university who was also a leader in the workplace, a leader of a workplace ministry, a business leader who now helps lead a campus ministry, and finally an expert on worldview. These chapters should be a tremendous resource for you as you look at your transition from several different viewpoints. These are folks who know what you are facing.

My prayer is that you will receive revelation from the Holy Spirit and that these truths will make a major impact on your life during this strategic time. May God use His Word, His Spirit, and these words to give you encouragement, wisdom, and hope.

"I BELIEVE IN THE REST OF THE STORY"

by Amy Kress

Transitioning from college is a winding journey filled with mixed emotions and uncertainties. You are not alone in your journey. Amy Kress, an InterVarsity alumna, allowed us to get a glimpse of what this transition was like in her blog.

May 14th, 2005

i'm going to graduate in like 13 hours. it's so weird. so weird. i totally don't feel like one of the big kids who has been here 4 years and is ready to leave. i mean, I am, but i'm not.

my stomach hurts. it's angst. i'm going to say goodbye to my friends of 4 years tomorrow. it's not the close friends that it will be hard to leave because i know i'll stay in touch, it's the people who i know kinda well who i'll miss. the people who never seemed to make much of a difference, but who have been a huge part of my time at college.

i'm graduating from college? i'm going to talk about "when i was in college..." isn't that the weirdest thing ever? i think so.

then there's the whole boy dimension. i thought when i was a freshman and sophomore that i'd totally find Mr. Right here at the college. well, i didn't. i didn't even come close! now, the weird thing is that i look around and see a few guys that i think, "he's pretty cool, i would totally go on a date with him if he asked me" but he's not asking. and i'm not going. and i'll probably never see him again. isn't that weird? i think it's very weird. *(See Chapter 9, Life is Brief)*

is it really over?

June 28th, 2005

can i seriously work at a desk for the rest of my life? i'm beginning to wonder... *(See Chapter 3, The Right Fit, Finding Your Best Job)*

July 8th, 2005

i love fridays and they love me! all week i've been really looking forward to the weekend and i'm not really sure why.

last night i rented *Office Space.* It was really beyond any of my wildest expectations. a corporate loser with his geek friends. between from my experience at my last few jobs, i could relate more than I want any of you to know.

July 11th, 2005

does anybody out there have a budget for managing your money? if so, do you have any tips for me, somebody who needs to start being more conscientious about money? *(See Chapter 8 on Dollars and Sense)*

July 31st, 2005

i'm trying not to freak out. this changing of life-seasons,
this shifting of priorities. moving home is exciting and
scary and mundane and weird all at once. i suppose any
new step after college is like that. there are just so many
unknowns: will i find a job that i enjoy? will i find a church
where i can fit in? will i have friends who will talk about
heart stuff, the gospel, ideas? will i become self-motivated
to paint and run and read when there's no one
around? *(See chapter 4 on Worshipping Together)*

August 7th, 2005

ahem. the interviews. *(See chapter 2 on Getting Started)*

well, they were all technically portfolio reviews which
means that you just march in, show your stuff, ask about
the company and leave your portfolio in hopes that the
next time they're hiring, they'll remember you and you'll
have an edge since they've already seen your stuff.

pretty much everyone told me i needed to learn web
(websites, multimedia, flash, etc.) to be more marketable.
i heard from several people that they could tell i hadn't
been to design school but that i had a good sense of
type, negative space, etc but that my work lacked
complexity.

so the plan is to move back home, keep showing this
portfolio to other places, get some sort of a job

(starbucks? waitressing at caffe anticoli? a lame 9-5er?) and take a flash, indesign, web, or identity class at sinclair or SAA, keep building the portfolio. i'm also going to head south to cinci and see what the job market looks like there.

August 19th, 2005

i just got asked (for the second time this week) where I see myself in 5 years. and i don't know!

ideally, i'd like to be married, working a job that will be interesting enough to make me get out of bed in the morning, hanging out with cool friends. but since i really can't control the first factor, i'd like a decent job and some buddies.

of course, they were asking career-wise, but i feel like i don't know myself well enough yet to know what i'd like. and even if i do know what i want, can i get there from here? and how long will that take? i don't know where i want to be geographically either. *(See Chapter 7 on Coming Alive, Finding Your Passion)*

maybe knowing where i'll be in 5 weeks is the more pressing question

September 3rd, 2005

i feel like I am at a train station in a foreign country. i feel like there are a million trains going all these different directions and i'm need to get on one, but i don't know exactly where it's going and i'm afraid i missed my connection somewhere back there but i can't be sure because no one speaks my language and no one knows where i'm ultimately trying to go (including me). *(See Chapter 6 on Finding a Mentor)*

September 10th, 2005

my brief visit to my college was interesting. my overall impression was that of looking through a glass door into a room i can never enter again. it was cool to see people, but i feel like i've changed so much since being in college. my priorities have shifted (GPA? wha?), my values are different (sleep is king).

i live at a much slower pace and i try to take more time to think and rest and i'm much less concerned with relationship drama. i wish i was able to connect with more alumni. i wonder how many of us are in food service? haha. or are pursuing "higher education"--does community college count? *(See Chapter 5 Searching for Community)*

October 28th, 2005

this afternoon i read through some old journals. it's a little weird how much i journal. i have 2/3rds of a bookshelf full of my thoughts, dreams, fears, feelings, and prayers since my freshman year of high school. pretty crazy to see how i've changed. i guess it was encouraging. not that i've arrived or anything, but i feel like i've learned a lot about people and myself and how to love and be honest and move through the sucky and beautiful parts of life.

Feb 6th, 2006

well, my friday of doom turns out to not have been very doom-ful. i got my job, my internship, and other stuff worked out, too, despite my paranoia.

i start work on wednesday, so tomorrow is my last day of loafing around. i may work on that painting since it's currently very ugly and hiding in the corner of my room. and i may try to read some more of the ragamuffin gospel--i got stuck around the middle. and i'll probably work on the freelance poster i'm doing for a symphony concert.

do any of you think it seems like february came awfully fast?

February 21st, 2006

i have a hard time calling myself an adult. does anyone else out there feel this way?

Thursday, March 23, 2006

i graduated from college 10 months ago. since then, i've
- taken 5 college classes and held 3.5 jobs
- travelled to egypt
- had my hair 3 colors
*- made a few trips to Grand Rapids
- found an interesting, intellectual, innovative group of cool friends who all have cool hair
- painted and redecorated my room
- acquired a taste for country music
- put thousands of miles on my car

- went to a conference that helped me decide to not go to grad school
*- freaked out. about everything.
- reworked my resume about 10 times
- slept in a lot
*- transitioned from being a multi-platform girl to a mac snob
- began a rad workout class that includes pilates, yoga, cardio, and "body sculpting" with several hilarious middle-aged ladies
- faithfully attended at a baptist church, a non-denom church (with southern baptist roots and ADD-inspired worship services), and a reformed episcopal church
- thought a lot about the essence of Christianity, what true faith is and looks like, how the gospel may transform my culture, and about what the Kingdom really is *(See Chapter 1, Tag You Are it!)*
- read don miller, john eldredge, kallistos ware, richard foster, madeline l'engle.

April 25th, 2006

today 4 high school students came to our office to present some design projects that my boss had them create through a class they're enrolled in at the career technology center. one of the vapieces was pretty good, but the rest were, you know, amateurish--nothing really ugly, but, you know not good either. so my boss had a "panel" of six of us come and critique their work. at one point, my boss had all of the kids leave and I, as the only woman in the room (after having been sent to get pens for everyone) said that we had to be nice to the poor guys. they all laughed at me and said i hadn't worked there long enough, but all i could remember was my emotionally-scarring first portfolio review. in the end, they all said a little something nice, even if it was completely insincere. i heaped compliments to compensate. when they left, everyone made fun of them.

November 13th, 2006

i had a really wonderful weekend.
cleaned
cooked some amazing food watched casablanca as the snow fell
spent over 6 hours on the phone with far-away friends
took a walk
went to church
*slept a lot
shoveled the sidewalk
*slid home from work friday
*gave myself brain cancer from talking to my boyfriend
*played a question game with lots of strangers
threw snowballs at my friend's apartment windows.
looked at overpriced coats.
discovered a shortcut downtown where i always get lost

...and generally had a delightful time. how 'bout you?

This article is taken from InterVarsity Christian Fellowship's, FLUX 2007 by Amy Kress. Used with permission of InterVarsity Christian Fellowship, USA, PO Box 7895 Madison WI, 53707 www.intervarsity.org/alumni

Amy Kress graduated from Hillsdale College and is currently working as a graphic designer.

CHAPTER ONE
Tag-You're it!

"Now all these things are from God, who reconciled us to Himself through Christ and gave us the ministry of reconciliation, namely, that God was in Christ reconciling the world to Himself, not counting their trespasses against them, and He has committed to us the word of reconciliation. Therefore, we are ambassadors for Christ, as though God were making an appeal through us; we beg you on behalf of Christ, be reconciled to God."

2 Corinthians 5:18-20

"As an extrovert, I'm still learning how to spend my time when I'm alone. It's important to find one or two hobbies to do outside of work. Pursue your passion, and you'll make friends along the way."*

Rob

You have been called by God to be His special representative in your sphere of influence. From before the foundation of the world He has had a design for your life. He has spent your entire lifetime preparing you for this time. He has carefully crafted your heritage, your background, your talents, your circumstances, your family situation, your friendships, your education, your training, and your role models to give you all that you need to be fully prepared to be an ambassador for Him. A few of your classmates are going to join the campus ministry, or go to seminary, or go into missions. God will use them in these ministries. However, what you need to fully understand is that God has special plans for you also. He has appointed you to be a "full-time" ambassador for Him. You will receive your salary not from the church or a Christian organization but from the marketplace.

Remember the question that will be our overriding focus:

"In this time of your transition, how do you <u>obey</u> His command to make disciples and to <u>represent</u> and glorify Him, in order that many may believe?"

How will this begin to unfold over the next few months and years in your own life? Let me share with you a little of my own journey.

MY STORY

I felt the sincere "call of God" on my life when I was seventeen years of age. At that time, I thought that if someone really loved Jesus, then he or she had to become a missionary or a pastor. I did not think that I could make it as a missionary, so I thought that God must have called me to the pastoral ministry. I entered a secular university in my home state, planning to go on to seminary after graduation. I was encouraged to take ten hours of Greek my freshman year. I also took science, English, and history, while ignoring my favorite subjects of math and business. I was "suffering for Jesus" by following the "calling of God". By my sophomore year I was nearly flunking out of school. I met with a young man who worked with students at another campus, and we spent a Saturday morning together. He shared with me that I could go into business, appropriate my talents and experiences, and still be used by Christ. The next day I switched my major to business, and my grades rose. It was easy for me, and I enjoyed nearly every class.

That was over 40 years ago, and my life has never been the same. Once I understood that I could still deeply love Jesus, yet be in the business world, my life blossomed with opportunities. If I had become a pastor, I would have been very average and frustrated in that position. Yet, as a business leader, my platform has allowed me to share Christ with my co-workers, customers, vendors, and competitors. I have been able to encourage marketplace leaders across the U.S. and around the globe. I shudder to think what would have happened to me had I not had that Saturday morning conversation in 1965. It was a defining moment in my life when I realized that I had been "called by God" to be in the distribution business in the workplace as a full-time representative and ambassador for the King of Kings.

DUALISM

For centuries we have lived under the curse of "Dualism". This has led to a secular / sacred divide. We have compartmentalized our lives into the spiritual and the worldly. Church and Christian activities are put into the "spiritual or religious" compartment, and the rest of our lives are considered "worldly". This is not how God intended for us to think. A friend of mine once said that the "spiritual" or "religious" things that we do become "secular" if they are done for the temporal, and the "secular" activities that we are involved in become "spiritual" if done for the eternal. So the key to whether something is spiritual is not which activity you are doing, but your purpose in doing it.

All of life is to be integrated and devoted to walking with Him and service to Him. I saw this in a recent visit to China. I was in Beijing attending a conference of Christian business leaders. While sharing in a small group, one young female executive said, "I cannot discuss my business with my pastor because he says that it is dirty." Another small business owner shared, "I cannot discuss my business with my church because it is worldly." My heart was grieved. Not only had we shared the gospel with our Chinese brothers and sisters, but we have passed on our wrong dualistic thinking that has so pervaded our churches.

If your Bible is close by, then turn to Hebrews 11. There we find the "Hall of Faith", where many of the great men and women of God are listed. It is interesting that most of these were regular people, just like you and me. They were not priests or prophets, but were in every kind of position in the workplace. Noah was in the construction business, Abraham, Isaac, and Jacob were shepherds, Joseph was a government leader, and Moses was a political leader. Rahab was a prostitute; what is she doing there? Gideon was a military leader, Samson was a judge, and David was a king. Yes, Samuel was a prophet, but he was in the minority. We can take great encouragement in the fact that these men and women were greatly used by God in every sector of society. They were not "second-class citizens" but were fully engaged in representing God in their positions of leadership.

As I visit and speak in churches around the world, I find that up to 80 percent of people in the pew feel that the "professionals" are to do the ministry. They have proverbial shackles on their ankles, handcuffs on their wrists, and blinders on their eyes. They do not feel that they are responsible for the ministry, but think that they are to pray and pay for the professionals to get it done. The fact is that it is the person in the congregation, rather that the person on the platform, that has the contact with those who do not know Christ. On Sunday only 17% of Americans will attend church, but on Monday morning a full one-hundred percent of them will be in the workplace, schools, and neighborhoods. You will be around more lost people in one day in the workplace than your pastor will encounter in a full week. God has placed you to be salt and light in your sphere of influence as His special representative.

FROGS AND LIZARDS

Years ago I was at a world-wide congress on evangelism in Manila (Lausanne, 1989). A few business leaders had a small part on the program with pastors, missionaries, church leaders, and seminary professors from all over the world. A Hong Kong stock broker, Lee Yih, was given the responsibility of sharing our thoughts as the workplace representatives. You will enjoy Lee Yih's analogy; **"*Frogs and Lizards-Why more and more of the best ministers are lay people*".**

"Have you ever noticed how differently frogs and lizards acquire their food? The frog sits and waits for the food to come to him. When an unlucky insect happens to fly by, he simply sticks out his tongue and reels it in. If the lizard sat around like the frog, however, he would starve to death. So he goes out into his world and hunts.

Now the frog in this analogy is the Vocational Christian Worker. He goes off to seminary, gets a degree, and goes on staff somewhere. Before you know it, ministry opportunities are coming to him and he has his hands full. In fact, when big frogs come to town, they have to hide in hotel rooms, or they'll be swamped.

The lizard, on the other hand, is a layperson. Ministry does not come seeking him out. Instead, he must move around in his environment, assess his sphere of influence, establish friendships, serve people, and once he has earned the right to be heard, be ready to give an account for the hope that is in him.

I think the main problem today in world evangelization is the under-utilization of the lizard. And a big part of the problem lies with the frog. Let's face it; he has a tendency to steal the show.

What's more, the layperson looks at the Vocational Christian Worker and says to himself, "I can never be as great as that." And he's probably right—as long as he defines ministry in frog terms!

The lizard needs to know how God can use him as the lizard that he is. And when he catches that vision, when he learns that evangelism is not an event but a process, and when he tastes the joy of seeing a friend find the Savior, he'll never want to give the ministry back to the frog again!"

I thought that many of the attendees who had key religious positions would be offended. However, they laughed and enjoyed the analogy. They would say in the hallways, "I am only a frog who gets to equip the lizards!" Yet, now over twenty years later, we still have this wrong perception that the "professional" has a special place in God's kingdom and that we are not as useful in God's service. As a "lizard" going into the workplace, you will every day be able to get into places that the "frog" can never go. Proverbs 30:28 tells us that lizards can be found in the palaces of kings. You will be able to squeeze into small places and seize opportunities for the Master in your workplace as a "lizard" representing Him.

THE PRIESTHOOD OF EVERY BELIEVER

We need to have a thorough understanding of the Priesthood of the Believer. My friend, David Dawson, has done a great job of explaining how we got off track in this area in his book, *"The Priesthood of Every Believer, Resolving the Clergy / Laity Distinction"*. In it he reminds us that we are a holy priesthood (I Peter 2:5) and a royal priesthood (I Peter 2:9). We have been chosen and ordained by Him (John 15:16) and are kings and priests (Revelation 1:6). The pastors and teachers are to be equipping the saints to do the work of the ministry (Ephesians 4:11, 12). We are not to be just assisting them in "their" ministry inside the walls of our churches, but they are to equip us to do the ministry that God has given us to do out where we live, work, and play everyday. Our focus is not to be on building a church or a ministry, but upon building disciples for Jesus Christ. Therefore, Christ is going to hold each of us responsible for going out and discipling the nations (Matthew 28:19, 20). Our churches are not there to entertain us or make us feel comfortable and encouraged. They are to be "equipping centers" to send us out into our world to evangelize and disciple and produce lasting spiritual fruit.

If you understand the importance of your calling and the dangers of dualistic thinking, then you will be way ahead of most of your peers. Your life will be fulfilled because you will be comfortable, secure, and at peace about what God has asked you to do with your life. The feelings of guilt and insecurity will be replaced by confidence and a simple trust in His provision for every detail of your life. Every day you will wake up with purpose and be filled by the Holy Spirit to impact those lives which He has sovereignly placed in your path.

You may want to get my book, *"Christ@Work Opening Doors, Impacting Your Workplace for Jesus Christ"*. It is filled with real life stories and practical tips on how to do evangelism and discipleship in the workplace. For those of you who want even more information in a larger book, get *"Show and then Tell, Presenting the Gospel in Daily Encounters"*, by Kent and Davidene Humphreys, published by Moody Press. You can visit our web site for power points, free audios, and other resources at www.lifestyleimpact.com

Questions for Discussion:

1. How would you define "dualism"?

2. Does there tend to be a "secular / sacred divide" in our lives? If so, how can we have an integrated life?

3. What ways does the lizard analogy fit into your current workplace?

4. What is your definition of the "Priesthood of Believers", and how can we be more intentional in our churches to be equipping ALL the saints for the ministry?

**Rob's quote and quotes for chapters 2 through 9 were taken from InterVarsity Christian Fellowship's, FLUX 2006. Used with permission of InterVarsity Christian Fellowship, USA, PO Box 7895 Madison WI, 53707 www.intervarsity.org/alumni

CHAPTER 2
Getting Started, Finding Your Place

"And He went out about the third hour and saw others standing idle in the <u>market place</u>; and to those He said, 'You also go into the vineyard, and whatever is right I will give you.' And so they went."

Matthew 20:3-4

"Then they said, "Let us arise and build." So they put their hands to the <u>good work</u>. . . I also applied myself to the work on this wall; we did not buy any land, and all my servants were gathered there for the <u>work</u>."

Nehemiah 2:18; 5:16

"I'm still adjusting from the always demanding but flexible schedule of a student to working 9 to 5, with the only flexibility being on evenings and weekends."

Grete

Some of you will be going to graduate school, but you will be working part time. Others of you will be going to medical school or law school or other training. Some of you have spent your summers going to camp, playing sports, taking vacations, or going on summer mission trips. If that is the case, you are entering the workplace for the <u>first time</u>. Other readers may have been working part-time jobs since you were 10 or 12 years of age. If you are a student who has worked during the summers, or even part time during the school year, you are much more prepared to enter the workplace. **If this is true of you, then you may just want to <u>scan this list</u> and move on to the next chapter**. But, before you leave this chapter, ALL of you should look closely at suggestions # 1, 5, 6, 9, and 10. Those specific suggestions will still be important even for those of you who are veterans in the job market.

As you review these suggestions, remember the question that you must constantly keep before you as you begin this new phase of your life:

"In this time of your transition, how do you <u>obey</u> His command to make disciples and to <u>represent</u> and glorify Him, in order that many may believe?"

TEN SUGGESTIONS FOR EARLY JOBS

1. Make a good first impression.

When you go to interviews, be prompt, well-groomed, and dressed appropriately. The workplace is much more casual today than just a few years ago. However, the experts tell us that it is better to overdress during an interview because that shows that you care. Be a good listener and try to pick up what is important to the person with whom you are talking. Keep your answers short. Be positive about former supervisors or workplaces. Be yourself, and be open about your background, your dreams, and your desire to serve and be a part of the team. Be confident of your talents, background, and accomplishments. Prepare ahead of time and find out as much as you can about the organization before your appointment. With company web sites available, this will be an easy thing for you to do. Your prior preparation will show that you want to be an informed applicant. Show a genuine desire to get the job. Treat the administrative people with care because they can help make the process much easier for you. Finally, ask the interviewer how you may follow up, and then keep in contact until a decision is made. Employers want to hire those who are passionate about joining their team. <u>Daniel</u> modeled this principle while a teenage slave in a foreign country. And he continued to do this as he served as the key advisor to four kings over a period of nearly 70 years.

2. Take jobs while in school.

Part-time jobs while in school or on summer vacations provide great opportunities to learn about various fields and industries. They also provide valuable contacts. Many summer interns end up getting the best jobs when they graduate. And the experience looks great on a resume. You will not only make money but will gain valuable insights into what you like to do. Be responsible. Work hard, work smart, and have a great attitude!

3. Don't shun the less desirable jobs.

Most early jobs are not that glamorous. Many are very routine, lowpaying, unrewarding, and not very difficult. But many future leaders start in those places and are noticed by their superiors. Learn a trade or profession in order to make a living while training for your most desired profession.

4. Start at the bottom.

You may be able to work your way up the ladder even in these early part-time jobs. Most large firms can always use another good leader. Bright, hardworking, aggressive, and responsible people will be promoted. It does not take long to distinguish yourself, particularly in a firm that is growing. In a bureaucratic firm with a lot of politics, you could get lost. So, be careful not to get stuck in a culture that does not reward good workers.

5. Be aggressive in your job search.

Examine all opportunities, even those that may appear beneath your ability or education. Those who sit by the phone or the computer waiting for just the right job will find that others have taken it. Usually, as a new graduate, you do not find your "perfect job". Remember, in most cases your degree just gets you in. Once on the job, you will have to prove yourself and show that you are special. Within a few months or years you will set yourself apart from your co-workers. Many times it will be "who you know" that helps you get into the right fit. The older you get, the more important relationships will be. Particularly in positions of leadership, your track record and long-term relationships will open the doors. People want to place those they can trust into critical positions. Paul started many of the early churches with the leaders that he had personally trained. Most executive job searches come down to key relationships, not just qualifications.

6. Gain experience everywhere that you can.

If you cannot find a job within a few weeks, it will be much better if you find a part-time or temporary position. Employers do not like to hire people that have been sitting around for months waiting for the right job. Besides, you may want to eat, and employment always helps with that! Get into the industry where you want to be and begin to establish contacts. Peter was always willing to try anything. Peter had many flaws, but an abundance of energy, and God shaped him into becoming the leader of the early church.

7. Give a little bit extra.

Arrive about 15 minutes early and stay a few minutes late. You will suddenly put yourself in the top 10% of your co-workers. Just that little bit will be noticed by observant supervisors. Ambition, eagerness, and willingness to make sure that the task is finished will be noticed. Jesus noticed the <u>women</u> that prepared the meals, washed His feet, and touched His garment. These women stood by Him as most of his disciples fled. If you want to be noticed by those in control, you have to do the little things.

8. Take good care of your equipment and your workspace.

Your employer may have a lot invested in the equipment that you are using, treat it like it is your own. You will probably be much better with technology than some of your older co-workers. Be a servant and help them to be more productive with their computer or technology. <u>Esther</u> followed all the rules and earned the respect of the king. When the crises came, Esther had the platform to be able to request a favor from the king because he had such respect for her. Your employer will watch how responsible you are. He will reward and promote those who are looking out for his best interests.

9. Make your supervisor a success.

If you look out for your superior, then you will be rewarded many times over. Loyalty is always rewarded. The only time that you can not support your superiors is when they lack integrity. Otherwise, you need to help them with the mission and make them look good. The workplace is all about relationships and others will notice how loyal and helpful you are to your supervisor. If you have different ideas about how to do things, then always present them with tack and creativity. Make sure that you have proven yourself first. Do not be a young "know it all". Remember they have been around for years and things are not always as simple or easy as they seem to a newcomer. <u>Joshua</u> served Moses for forty years before he assumed leadership of the children of Israel.

10. Learn how to be a servant and understand the value of a TEAM

Be helpful to your co-workers. Take out the trash. Do the things that others do not want to do. Listen to your co-workers and learn about their families and their lives. Be available to help others in their project or little chore. Look out for the interests of others, and you will always have people wanting you on their team. David was a servant leader that his men greatly respected.

You may say that these ten suggestions are simple and should be automatic. However, I have found after years of supervising hundreds of employees, that most of those employees did not even follow these basic principles. By just practicing the above simple suggestions, you will put yourself in the top half of all employees. The next stage is to get into the top 20% of the employee base, which will not be hard for you to do. Every firm is dependent upon the top 20% of their most faithful and loyal employees. The middle 60% will follow the lead of the 20%. I have even found that you can remove the bottom 20% of the workers of any operation and lose very little productivity. So, establish yourself in the top 20% of the company's workforce as soon as you can. Then you will be given opportunities as you prove yourself.

Questions for Discussion:

1. What value have you found in the part-time jobs and internships that you have had during your college years?

2. You will have a much higher education than many of your new co-workers. Why is it sometimes difficult for us to humble ourselves to those who have not been given the opportunities that we have?

3. What are some tips that you have found helpful in securing your job that you could share with the rest of us?

4. Why are we so hesitant to try to make others successful? Do we think that it might endanger our own ambitions? Why?

CHAPTER 3
The Right Fit - Finding Your Best Job

"When our enemies heard that it was known to us, and that God had frustrated their plan, then all of us returned to the wall, each one to his work

...So I sent messengers to them, saying, 'I am doing a great work and I cannot come down. Why should the work stop while I leave it and come down to you?'"

Nehemiah 4:15; 6:3

"Do you see a man skilled in his work? He will stand before kings; He will not stand before obscure men."

Proverbs 22:29

"I took my job believing that it would be a great experience to 'get my foot in the door'. I did feel called to my position for a time by the Lord for very specific reasons, but I also can't deny that now He is calling me to something else. I'm confident in my decision to leave because I'm confident in Him, and I know that there's something out there that He created me for."

Marie

You will spend most of your waking hours in your workplace or traveling to and from the job, so it is more than just a source of income. Much of your identity and satisfaction in life will come from your job, so it needs to be a good fit. If you are like most graduates, you may even find that

41

your first job is in a field that is not exactly what you studied for in the university. You may be graduating at a time of economic uncertainty, or there may be a surplus of job seekers in your field. This is a time to be flexible and alert to what God is preparing for you in this season of your life. Now that we have covered the basics that most of you have learned in your early jobs and part-time employment, let me share with you twelve principles that will be very helpful for you as you leave the campus and go into the workplace fulltime.

Remember the question that you must ask yourself as you ponder God's definition of success in your life and in your workplace:

"In this time of your transition, how do you <u>obey</u> His command to make disciples and to <u>represent</u> and glorify Him, in order that many may believe?"

Twelve Suggestions for Success in the Workplace

1. Attitude is always more important than ability.

After spending a lot of money and several years of your life getting a college education, you may doubt the above statement. However, after you enter the workplace and get around some very bright and talented co-workers with bad attitudes, you will quickly agree with me. A leadership team can always use someone who may not the brightest or the most capable, if they have a great attitude. If someone has great talent, but is impossible to work with and is always stirring up strife, it seldom works out. That one person can destroy a team or a company culture in no time at all. Proverbs 15:30 tells us, *"Bright eyes gladden the heart; Good news puts fat on the bones."* And Philippians 2:14-15 reminds us, *"Do all things without grumbling or disputing; so that you will prove yourselves to be blameless and innocent, children of God above reproach in the midst of a crooked and perverse generation, among whom you appear as lights in the world."* Your employer is going to assume that you have a good education. What they want to see in you is that you have a great attitude which will blend in with their culture. It starts by you coming in with a humble servant attitude and be willing to listen and learn. You do not have to impress them with what you know. You need to show them who you are.

A <u>positive</u> attitude can brighten even the most difficult work situations. Some of my co-workers thought that my favorite time of the week was Monday morning. I always looked forward to my work with anticipation. I strive to remain positive even when we face great difficulties. I have learned the principle: God is in control and has my best interests at heart. He is sovereign, all-powerful, all-knowing, and He loves me. How can I not be encouraged knowing that?

So, be alert, cheerful, prompt, and caring. When you exemplify these characteristics, you will always have people wanting to be on your team. Proverbs 15:13, 15 reminds us of this eternal principle, *"A joyful heart makes a cheerful face, But when the heart is sad, the spirit is broken…All the days of the afflicted are bad, But a cheerful heart has a continual feast."* Positive people make great co-workers and long-term employees. It is one of the key things that ensures good job security.

2. Work hard.

Realize that there is no substitute for hard work. That does not mean that we do not also work smart. You will find, however, that most of your co-workers only do what is required. You want to be like Joseph or Daniel, who amazed their superiors.

43

Proverbs 14:23 says, *"In all labor there is profit, But mere talk leads only to poverty."* Many new grads can talk a good game. What your employer wants to see from you is that your actions back up what you say. Many of your fellow employees did not have the privilege of getting a college education. So you may have to prove to them that you can "get your hands dirty" and get the job done. They will be valuable assets to you as you take more responsibility and take ownership of team projects. I remember when my son, Lance, came into our family business straight out of college. He had to work in every area of the distribution firm over the first few years. He was respected by the fork lift drivers, truck drivers, and warehouse stockers because he sat down with them for lunch. He was not afraid to get his hands dirty and do any job. He gained their respect by his actions and you can believe that they were closely watching the boss's son!

3. Be reliable.

Be a man or a woman of your word. Reliability means everything. Proverbs 20:6 is familiar to many of you. *"Many a man proclaims his own loyalty, but who can find a trustworthy man?"* In the workplace, everyone is looking for people that they can trust. Your reputation will be one of the most important things that you have. (However, God is teaching me that He is more concerned with my character and what He knows, versus what others think of me.) With our vendors, our customers, and our employees, we established a track record of being dependable. Others knew that whatever we promised, we would do. We later found out that major retailers did not forget our reputation for being trustworthy. Even fifteen to twenty years later, others will remember that you are a person of your word. Do not sacrifice your reputation. It will pay big dividends as you go through life. Besides, even if it did not, you want to honor God by being a trustworthy individual.

4. Be honest.

Honesty is required by God and demanded by those in authority. It allows you to have a clear conscience. Honesty is manifested in the little things, like how we handle supplies, how we justify our expenses, and how thoroughly we present our reports. Jesus talked about this in Luke 16:10-12, *"He who is faithful in a very little thing is faithful also in much; and he who is unrighteous in a very little thing is unrighteous also in much. Therefore, if you have not been faithful in the use of unrighteous wealth, who will entrust the true riches to you? And if you have not been faithful in the use of that which is another's, who will give you that which is your own?"* Be careful not to use exaggeration in dealing with customers or your superiors. Exaggeration is a form of dishonesty, as is withholding the truth in order to leave a false impression.

5. Do not create needs, fill them.

Never try to educate the client or customer and tell them what they need. Just find out what they want and get it for them. It took me many years to apply this lesson, even though my father taught it to me while I was a young man learning the distribution business,. I was enthusiastic about our products and services, so, many times I talked instead of listening to my customers. Finally, I not only learned to listen to my retailers and their needs, but also learned to understand the needs of the final consumer. Meeting the needs of others will always provide a good living for you. You will be very successful in your work if you find ways to meet the physical, emotional, social, mental, and spiritual needs of others. I have lost a lot of money by trying to educate the consumer, but by studying their wants and needs, my efforts became profitable. Listen to your client, your customer, and your consumer; good listeners will be rewarded with sales, opportunities, and profits. Jesus was constantly meeting the physical, emotional, and spiritual needs of those that he encountered. As a result, He had followers wherever He went.

6. Specialize.

Specialists tend to make more money and have better job security. This is true in medicine, in law, and in most professions. At times I have been a successful entrepreneur because I understand the big picture and how all the pieces fit together. We carried 12,000 items in our distribution business, but we made most of our profits on a few hundred. The top twenty percent of your products will always produce 80% of your sales and profits. We grew because we specialized in a few categories of products. Do something that most others cannot do well. Separate yourself from the masses. Do the most difficult, the most challenging – the tasks that others do not want to do. Find a niche and be the very best at that product, or service, or area of expertise.

7. Provide value, but make a profit.

Make sure that you provide <u>value</u> for your customer. You want to give them a good value for what they pay. However, never try to be the lowest cost service or lowest cost product. Someone else can and will always charge a lower price. They may eventually go bankrupt, but in the meantime, they will run you out of business. So, charge a reasonable price for your product or service, but give them value and excellent service. If the customer, client, or consumer values what you offer, they will pay a reasonable price. In every industry or service, most of the customers know which firms consistently provide the best values. Become an employee of that firm and learn that industry. Help your employer to continue to improve.

8. Plan ahead, keep your priorities, and stay organized.

Planning will save you many hours of extra work. Before you leave work each night, have your priorities set for the next morning. Plan your year, your month, and your week ahead of time. A few minutes of planning not only saves time, but it helps you avoid frustration and heartache. You can also save wasted time by keeping your desk in order and files organized. Successful people know where they are going and where the important documents are located. Those who are constantly running behind schedule, disorganized, and do not have their priorities in order are often not successful.

David presented detailed plans for the temple to his son Solomon in 1 Chronicles 28:11-12: *"Then David gave to his son Solomon the plan of the porch of the temple, its buildings, its storehouses, its upper rooms, its inner rooms and the room for the mercy seat; and the plan of all that he had in mind."*

As a wise man once said, "Plan your work, and then work the plan."

9. Realize that the most important asset of any firm is its people.

Therefore, value every person with whom you work. That means to not only value your peers, superiors, and your customers, but also the folks whose value tends to be overlooked. God values every person and treats them with dignity; we should do the same. I learned in the distribution business that the person who checked me in at the back door could be more important than the store manager. The clerk can make you or break you. The door man, the custodian, the truck driver, the secretary, the administrative assistant, and the lowest paid temporary worker are all unique people. Learn to value them, and you will be rewarded. They can quickly tell if you are looking down on them. Respect the wise older people that have been around forever.

They may not have your education, but their wisdom will be invaluable to you in your job.

Jesus understood this principle. He did not leave an organization, buildings, or a large treasury. He simply invested His life into a few men and women. Jesus knew that a few good people were the key to the success of taking the Good News to the entire world.

10. Get wisdom and learn from successful people-

The very best advice that you get will probably be free. Ask for free advice from the most successful people in your field. Look for those who are 50 or 60 or 70 years of age and have been around long enough to have had many failures and a few successes. We learn most from our failures, and you may as well not have to pay the high costs that they paid for their wisdom. They will gladly share with you what they have learned if you are humble, gracious, and show honor to them. They will love to tell the secrets that they have learned, but only if you ask them. They are looking for young people who have a dream and are willing to listen to the older generation. Of course, the best source of wisdom is God the Father and the Word of God. Next to that is the counsel of godly men and women.

Wisdom is mentioned over 200 times in Scripture and 50 times in Proverbs alone. Time after time we are told in Proverbs to seek wisdom and understanding. In Proverbs 2:2-10 we read, *"Make your ear attentive to wisdom, Incline your heart to understanding; for if you cry for discernment, lift your voice for understanding; if you seek her as silver and search for her as for hidden treasures; then you will discern the fear of the LORD and discover the knowledge of God. For the LORD gives wisdom; from His mouth come knowledge and understanding. He stores up sound wisdom for the upright; He is a shield to those who walk in* *integrity, guarding the paths of justice, and He preserves the way of His godly ones. Then you will discern righteousness and justice and equity and every good course. For <u>wisdom</u> will enter your heart, and knowledge will be pleasant to your soul."*

The writer of Proverbs constantly challenged us to get this wisdom:

Proverbs 3:13, *"How blessed is the man who finds <u>wisdom,</u> and the man who gains understanding."*

Proverbs 4:5, *"Acquire <u>wisdom!</u> Acquire understanding!"*

Proverbs 5:1, *"My son, give attention to my <u>wisdom,</u> Incline your ear to my understanding;"*

Proverbs 8:11, *"For <u>wisdom</u> is better than jewels; And all desirable things cannot compare with her."*

For the last few years you have paid a price in both money and time to gain a lot of knowledge. Now I am saying to you that the wisdom that you can gain free of charge will be available to you if you will only seek the Lord and ask wise counselors and mentors. We will spend more time on this subject in a later chapter.

11. Know yourself-

In order to be successful in the workplace and in life, you need to understand yourself. This will not be done easily or quickly. However, the better that you know yourself, the more effective you will be in your job and the more satisfied you will be in your life. This includes understanding your talents, your background, your gifts, your experiences, and your passions. See Romans 12, I Corinthians 12, and Ephesians 4. If you spend more of your time doing what you enjoy, then you will be much more productive. We will spend much more time on this in the chapter on **Coming Alive!**

I would strongly recommend that you go to www.crown.org and use their *Career Direct* program. It is a valuable tool in identifying your strengths as they relate to the workplace and specific careers. If you are not quite certain that you are heading the right direction, this resource could be a help to you. Also, in the appendixes of this book, I have a brief outline that will help you in finding **God's will for your life and career**. This appendix has numerous Scriptures that you can research to give you guidance in seeking God's will in the key decisions in your life.

12. Take Leadership-

Most of you have special gifts that will allow you to have a niche skill area. Although you may never be in a supervisory position over a large staff, you will always be in demand if you are good at what you do. You may be part of the 80% who will not be on the platform as a visible leader, but you are the ones that keep every firm moving forward in the day-to-day operations. In contrast, a <u>few of you</u> are generalists. People like us do not know enough about any one thing, so we have to be satisfied with leading those that do! If you are a strong, driven leader who will eventually want major responsibility over people and operations, start early. By age 30 to 40, you should be well on track for your career. By age 35 to 45, if that is your desire, you could have major responsibility, and by age 40 to 50, you could be in a key leadership position. But if not, remember that some millionaire entrepreneurs went broke several times and finally found success after 50 or even 60 years of age! Moses' training program as a leader lasted 40 years, and he started his responsibility at 80 years of age. Joseph's training lasted 13 years, and he took massive responsibility at only 30 years of age. Joseph (Genesis 37 to 50), Daniel (book of Daniel), and Joshua (book of Joshua) are great examples in this area of taking the responsibility of leading others. I would encourage you to examine their stories and learn from them. They are my favorite Bible characters and have been a great example for my life and ministry.

Please note that the above formulas worked for my older generation. Instead of having three or four major employers, you will probably have at least three to four major careers. This is NOT your parents or grandparents workplace. I am in my third different major career change in my sixties! So, being reliable will move you UP the corporate ladder, but YOU may decide after a while to move OUT to something new and different or to step out and do your own thing. My son and son-in-law are both 40 years of age and going into a second or third career transition after having excellent success in other fields. This is common today, so the key is for you to be flexible and look for what God has for you in a changing workplace. He will never waste your experiences from one period of life as you transition into the next. God's purpose is to prepare you for eternity and use you while you are on this earth to represent Him. The income or the possible worldly successes are only temporal benefits along the way to His eternal purposes for your life.

Questions for Discussion:

1. What are some ways that you have exhibited a positive attitude to your leaders and co-workers in the workplace?

2. Is it easy for you to stay organized on the job and keep up with your priorities? What are some tips that you have learned?

3. Have you been able to learn from successful people? How were you able to gather some of their wisdom?

4. What are your key talents, your spiritual gifts, and the driving passion of your life?

Chapter 4
Worshipping Together, Finding a Local Church Home

"In the early morning, while it was still dark, Jesus got up, left the house, and went away to a secluded place, and was praying there."

Mark 1:35

"Now during the day He was teaching in the temple, but at evening He would go out and spend the night on the mount that is called Olivet. And all the people would get up early in the morning to come to Him in the temple to listen to Him."

Luke 21:37-38

"It was difficult after moving to a new area to find a church, and it's a really bad idea to try to find a perfect church. Otherwise, you wander from church to church, and you go through a period of being and feeling disconnected–from having all the friends you hang out with at college, to nothing."

Michael

As I was editing this chapter, I got a phone call from my good friend, "Paul". I met Paul three years ago when I spoke to a business group at a Christian university in a nearby town. I always invite the students to lunch if they want to know more about the workplace. Paul emailed me, and we met for lunch. Over the next two or three years, we met several times a year. Paul is one of the brightest young entrepreneurs that I have known in forty years in business. He had started two or three small businesses before even graduating from college. Paul graduated four months ago; two months later, he moved from Oklahoma to the west coast to work for a large firm. He just called today to ask for my advice about buying a condo and how to pursue an idea that he has for the travel industry. Then he mentioned that one of his key issues is finding a church home in the new large city. Out of 25 co-workers in his workplace, only one is a follower of Christ. Paul had excellent training on his campus, has a heart for God, and wants to fellowship with other like-minded believers. However, finding that new fellowship in a large secular city is a real challenge. So I am going to look through my contacts and connect Paul with some Christian workplace leaders in his area that can help him in his walk with God, in finding a church home, and in finding a mentor to guide him during these first critical years in the workplace.

When college graduates from the best Christian university campuses and the best student ministries leave their campuses and move away to take a new job, they seldom find a church quickly. In fact, some of them do not really get involved in a local church for months or even years. For some, it is just that their lives are in huge transition, changing in location, career, perhaps marriage, and other areas. These grads look for a church or ministry that is similar to the one they had on their campus, and they have difficulty finding it. The music may be the same, but the preaching is different. Or, there just does not seem to be a lot of singles their age or young couples that are compatible. They may be traveling with friends on the weekends or going back home to see the folks and just never seem to get into a routine. Regardless of the causes, we, as the Body of Christ, are losing a number of students in the process.

Many students eventually get married and have children, and only then find their way back into the organized church. They want to share their Christian values with their children, but this may be five to seven years later, and the flame that once burned brightly in their hearts has been nearly put out. Because these young adults are struggling with so many adjustments, the activities and priorities which held such a high priority in college get put on the back burner and ignored. This often leads to guilt, but little change. Therefore, the Body of Christ is losing some of the fruit of campus ministries. If this were a for-profit business, the investors would look for ways to conserve the fruits of their long-term investments. While many campus ministries are able to spend a lot of time and energy with those graduates that decide to go on "full-time" staff, or those who stick around the campus for a job, or even the key leaders who move to the workplace, they simply do not have the staff or resources to keep track of the majority of you who move to another city.

While you may have received a lot of spiritual training on the campus, you may now realize that you had more time at school than you have now for relationships, evangelism, discipleship, and growing in your own walk with God. For those few years you were in a sheltered environment in a time of concentrated learning. Now you are bombarded by demands from the job, establishing your own household, learning to be responsible for all of your finances, perhaps adjusting to a marriage, and maybe even learning to be a parent. The priority of finding that "perfect church" or "small group" of other like-minded followers of Jesus suddenly gets put near the bottom of the list.

I want to share with you four things that you must have in your life if you are to survive spiritually. We will cover two of them in this chapter and two of them in the next chapter. All four of these activities are modeled by Jesus in His last days and hours just before the cross. In Mark 13, we see Jesus teaching in the temple. He would often go to the temple and teach or have discussions with the religious leaders. Then, in Mark 14, we see Jesus gathered with the twelve disciples for the Passover meal. Judas leaves, and Jesus takes the remaining eleven to the garden. There, He asks Peter, James, and John to come with Him, and for the other eight to remain there. He takes the three into the garden and has them wait and pray. Finally, He goes a few steps forward and falls on His face before the Father.

As we begin to look at these <u>four</u> activities that will become a necessary foundation for your walk with God and relationships with others in His Body, we must continue to hold up the question that you must ask and the prayer of Christ for each of our lives:

"In this time of your transition, how do you <u>obey</u> His command to make disciples and to <u>represent</u> and glorify Him, in order that many may believe?"

FOUR KEY ACTIVITIES

Here we see the <u>four</u> activities that each of us is to have in our lives:

1. Large Group-

We each need to be involved in a large group to worship, like a local church. We need to be encouraged, and we need to be taught from God's Word. The local Body of Christ should be visible and available to us for our benefit and as we serve others.

2. Small Group-

Each of us needs to be involved in a small group of six to twelve others which meets on a regular basis. This is a practice that we will need to participate in for a lifetime. We will never outgrow our need for it.

3. Inner Circle-

When the storms of life come, and they will come for every one of us, we will need an "inner circle". This circle is comprised of two to four other people who care about our soul. They may live in another city, and it may take you several years to find them, but you will not be able to survive the crises of life without them. Who would you call in a crisis in the middle of the night? That will tell you what kind of friends that they need to be. You do not have to meet in a regular group with them or spend 24 hours a day with them like Jesus did, but you need to have a consistent intimate relationship with them, and work on that relationship over many years.

4. Time with God-

Finally, Jesus modeled time alone with God. If He needed that, as the Son of God, then how much more do we need it? Jesus often got away to a private place to spend time with His Father. In Mark 1:35 we read, *"In the early morning, while it was still dark, Jesus got up, left the house, and went away to a secluded place, and was praying there."*

You will not survive long term or finish well in the Christian life unless you incorporate each of these four activities into your life. I have found that those followers of Christ that just try to maintain one or two of these will not continue to walk with Him over the years. Let us now look closer at two of these four activities.

Time With God
Your Devotional Life

Let me say just a few things about your daily time with God. If you are like me, then when your schedule changes, or you are traveling, it is easy to put off your daily private time with the Father. I have been working on this for fifty years, and it remains a challenge. The weekends are hardest for me, and, for many years, Sunday was the most difficult, even though I had the most time that morning. I love my time in prayer and His Word, but I need to keep it fresh. I want to have a thirst to know God (Psalm 53:2). I have read the Bible through in many of those years. I have used the **One Year Bible** and many other versions. I particularly like **The Living Bible** and **The Message,** which are paraphrases, but make the Word come alive. The best thing you can do for your career is to get into God's Word, every day, and gain His wisdom. Psalms 119:105 promises us, *"Your word is a lamp to my feet and a light to my path."* Go to that Psalm and reread it again. You will find that God's Word is mentioned in nearly every verse.

I also like to use one or two devotional books to challenge my thinking along with the Bible. My favorite is *"My Utmost for His Highest"* by Oswald Chambers. It is a classic, written nearly 100 years ago. There are many other good books. Just get in the habit of establishing a place and a time. Do it early in the day, because if you wait until evening, your mind won't be as sharp; you will be tired and more likely to skip it. Try to meet God every day. Jesus is our example, as are Daniel (Daniel 6:10), and the Psalmist (Psalm 5:3; 42:1 & 2; 46:10).

Prayer was the most difficult thing for me. I was never good at lists or journals, so I started using 3 x 5 cards some 25 years ago. I have used the cards to pray as I walk around the track at the gym or use my exercise bike. I love to pray as I walk around the neighborhood. Keep your prayer life fresh and creative. You may want to use your cell phone or lap top or other technology to remind you of requests and friends that you need to bring before God's throne. God wants you to talk with Him throughout the day as well. Paul tells us in 1 Thessalonians 5:17, *"pray without ceasing."*

I also like to start my time of prayer by praising God for who He is. Years ago someone from Campus Crusade shared these attributes of God with me, and I memorized them. I have used them for the last 40 years, thousands of times. God is:

All Powerful	Love
All Knowing	Just
Present Everywhere	Perfectly Righteous
Sovereign	Truth
Eternal	Unchanging
Full of Grace	Merciful
Holy, Holy, Holy	

Large Group
Finding a Church Home

Priority

Today you have many options in many cities. This is particularly true in certain parts of the country. Some of you will be moving to smaller communities where the options are more limited or to parts of the country where churches are much different than those you have attended. In many cities, there are not only many denominations to choose from, but many churches which are a blend or independent. Yet even with all of these options, one veteran student ministry leader told me that about 50% percent of his graduates have major problems finding a good church home. The reason is that churches are like institutions and are very slow to change. So each generation has to form their own "wine skins" because they do not fit into the old ones easily. This means that you are really going to have to work on this and make it a <u>priority</u> as you make your move.

Variety

You can find every form of music, from traditional to the latest contemporary Christian hits from your generation. Our older generation appreciates all that you are continuing to teach us about praise and worship. As you search, you will probably find every type of service and preaching imaginable. However, I can promise you two things: there is NO "perfect church", so you may as well not look for it: and you will NOT be able to "change" a church to make it just like you want it. So, the best thing to do is to find one that is somewhat close to what you believe a church should be. The main thing is for you to start attending somewhere and become involved in a local Body of Believers.

Regularity

Find a church and attend the services regularly. Remember that it is where you are to be equipped to minister OUTSIDE the four walls of the building. Also, you should be active within the church in helping to equip others for the ministry to which God has called them. The primary thing to remember is to not give your life building that church or those programs; be a part of building up the saints, so that they can become **salt and light** where they live, work, and play. You cannot do everything in the church (although others will notice your gifts and ask you to do so), and if you do, then you will be of no use to God outside the walls. So, pick only one or two activities that will help you to grow in your walk with God. Then choose one way that you can serve the rest of the local Body. It should be a place where you can maximize your effectiveness through your spiritual gift. (We will talk more about that later.) Take the pastor or a staff member out to breakfast or lunch and share with them your background, training, passion, and what you want to do to fit in with what God is doing at that church. If you will contact our office or email me, I will send you my book to pastors and workplace leaders, *"Shepherding Horses, Understanding God's Plan for Transforming Leaders"*. This will help your pastor understand leaders like you and how he can relate to you and best serve you as you minister for Christ in your workplace.

Some of you, who are more non-traditional, may find yourself joining with some friends to start a new fellowship in which you will be comfortable. You may want to be a part of a "new church plant" or a "house church". These experiences will be very rewarding and different. Many students enjoy the challenge of planting a church in the inner city or a new area of town. Others enjoy the sweet close fellowship of a small house church that may or may not be connected with a larger congregation. The key is that you get regular time each week with other serious followers of Jesus Christ. You need time for hearing and studying God's Word as a group, for worship and praise, for praying together, for equipping, for serving other needs in the Body, and for reaching out together to impact your city for Christ.

So keep connected with your Heavenly Father daily through His Word, prayer, and continuing to be filled with His Holy Spirit. Get connected as soon as possible with a local church when you move to another city. Do not put it off; Satan will use your delay against you. You do not want the bright fire that is in your heart to grow cold or dim. Take your time and get the right local fellowship, but make a choice.

Questions for Discussion:

1. Have you struggled, as most of us have, in maintaining a consistent devotional life? Which times are the most difficult?

2. If this is strength in your life, what are some ways that you can share with us that have given variety and freshness to your prayer life, time in the Word, and intimacy with God?

3. What styles of corporate worship do you enjoy, and do you expect that these will be easy to find in your new city?

4. What are the three or four things that are most important as you seek to find a new church home in your time of transition?

CHAPTER 5

Searching for Community, Finding Your Peers

"And He __appointed twelve__, so that they would be with Him and that He could send them out to preach."

Mark 3:14

"Sitting down, He __called the twelve__ and said to them,..."

Mark 9:35

"And when day came, He called His disciples to Him and __chose twelve__ of them..."

Luke 6:13

"Then He __took the twelve aside__ and said to them..."

Luke 18:31

"And He took with Him __Peter and James and John__..."

Mark 14:33

"I miss my friends and the fellowship I had on campus. I had a lot of leadership responsibilities on campus, and now I don't lead anything."

Grete

One of the key words that God is emphasizing today is community. One experienced student minister called this "like-hearted friends". The Father has always wanted His children to be together in community. Six times in John 17, Jesus asks that we may be one. Jesus modeled community with the twelve during His three years of ministry with them.

One of the things that you experienced on the university campus was community. God wants you to continue to experience that as a regular part of your life until the day that you leave this world. You will never get too old to need the fellowship of other followers of Jesus on a regular basis. That is why I tell people that they need to be in a regular small group for the rest of their lives.

This community, or oneness, becomes the foundation for our unity that others will notice which will bring glory to Him. Remember our question:

"In this time of your transition, how do you obey His command to make disciples and to represent and glorify Him, in order that many may believe?"

THE SMALL GROUP

As I mentioned in the last chapter, there are four activities that will help you to survive and thrive in your walk with Christ. One is to be involved in a church, in a large group setting for worship and teaching. Jesus modeled this by going to the temple on a regular basis, then going out to the marketplace where He did most of his ministry. We discussed the importance of this in the last chapter.

Secondly, Jesus modeled the small group in His relationship with the twelve. You need to follow His example. You can find these groups in several places, including a Bible study organized by your church. Your church may have groups for singles, married couples, men, women, specific age groups, or groups meeting in various parts of your city. You may join a house church or cell group that may or may not be a part of your church. Or, you could join one of the thousands of small groups of believers that are meeting in office buildings, in factories, and in other workplaces across our nation. For six years I led the *Fellowship of Companies for Christ, International* (www.fcci.org), an organization that supports small groups of business owners and business leaders meeting weekly in 25 nations around the world. There are many good workplace organizations that have small groups for those in the workplace, some of which are listed in Appendix II. Today, many churches are recognizing the need to start groups out in the workplace. Most groups in the workplace are informal and started by people just like you. You can get resources from any of these listed workplace ministries, the campus and publishing ministries that we have listed under Small Group Resources, or from your local church.

Although some teaching occurs in small groups, that is not the primary focus. They are not primarily for prayer, although that is a key element. They are not just for fun and fellowship, although we certainly need that in our lives as well. These groups are the one place that we can be vulnerable and real and share our lives in an *accountable community*. Most Christians rarely take off their masks and reveal who they really are. We need one place that is safe and secure for us to share our true desires, dreams, fears, and challenges. This happens in a small group. The best size for interaction is somewhere between 6 and 12. When you get past 15 you lose the intimacy that is necessary to feel emotionally safe. When you drop below 5 or 6 you actually need more members to contribute to the discussion. The best length of time for a meeting is somewhere between 45 and 90 minutes. You may want to have the meeting with a meal or refreshments before or afterward.

The best time for your meeting depends on who is in the group. For your age, you may want to meet on a Sunday evening or on a weekday evening. You will probably find that most workplace groups meet in someone's office in the morning before work. Meeting weekly or bi-weekly works well. Every group needs to have at least four common elements: a form of teaching, a time of interaction and discussion, a time of sharing personal needs, and a time of group prayer. The teaching element can be a DVD, a discussion of a book, a small group Bible study, or simply reading the Scriptures together. The discussion should be led by a leader or a co-leader, and it should allow everyone to contribute and not be dominated by one person. The time of sharing needs to be brief so that everyone who wants to, can share a current situation or need. Finally, the time of group prayer should not be minimized and will be the one thing that bonds the group together. A length of time for the group to meet should be set at the beginning (for example, four months, nine months, etc.), followed by re-evaluation. Some members may want to join a different group at this time. I have noticed that if a group stays together for a year, it is likely that the friendships involved will grow and deepen, and a very long-time bond will be created. Such groups are very special indeed.

When you get to your new city, this should be one of your top priorities. It is probably more important than joining a local church or fellowship because you will experience community quicker in a regular small group. If you go to your church, your workplace, and other groups and cannot find the right small group, do not be discouraged. Just find one other follower of Jesus, meet with that person weekly, and begin to pray. Ask God to bring other names to mind that you could invite to the group. Make your list and pray over the names, then invite them for a first time meeting. Share with them your ideas for the group and listen to what the other participants are looking for. Share with the others what booklets, or studies, or themes could be the keys for the group. You can find many good resources from the campus ministries listed in the *Appendix* and others like Focus on the Family and Crown Financial Ministries. Your new small group will become one of the most vital and important activities of your new life and will come the closest to giving you the community that you had on the campus. Remember that life transformation rarely happens in a large group. Transformation happens in small groups and "one-on-one" relationships as we are challenged and held accountable by others to obey the Scriptures and apply God's Word to our lives.

YOUR INNER CIRCLE

Most Christians do not understand the need to have an "inner circle", even though Jesus modeled this principle with Peter, James, and John. You do not have to meet in a regular group with these two or three others or to spend 24 hours a day with them like Jesus did, but you need to have a consistent intimate relationship with them and work on that relationship over many years. Most of the time spent with members of your 'inner circle" will probably be "one-on-one" time over a meal, an activity, or over the phone. You will have <u>unique</u> relationships with each of your inner circle friends.

The example of Jesus is a model for us. For most men, this type of intimacy is very difficult. I am in South Africa as I write this chapter. One of the men shared at dinner last night that men here are tough, rugged individuals and rarely open up to other men. The same is true in the USA, except that we are a little more open. The Promise Keepers, a movement of men used by God in the last generation, helped this situation. God will use specific leaders and groups to emphasize this type of intimacy to your generation. Even though technology connects your generation in so many ways, there is still that genuine yearning for "face-to-face" intimacy with your peers. This desire for intimacy is from God and very healthy. All of us, men and women, need to have this intense personal fellowship in our lives. We need two or three others who care about our soul. These are the people that we would call at 2 a.m. when we have a crisis. With these close friends, we can be more open than we can in our small group.

It may take you a while to find three key people. For me it was a natural process over several years. Eventually I had two men and my wife, Davidene, who were my inner circle. A couple of years ago, Bruce, my closest friend, died at 59 years of age. Today, I have three men and Davidene who are constantly up to date with my life and challenges. The people may change over the years as you move and go through the seasons of life, but always be alert to who God wants you to have in your inner circle. They may not all live in your city or state. They do not need to meet together on a regular basis, and they may not even know the others. You are the one who has a personal relationship with each one of them. These men and women will be the keys to your growth and accountability for the difficult areas of your life, like finances, moral purity, spiritual pride, and career decisions. They are there to counsel you, ask the hard questions, and hold you accountable when others do not have the courage to do so. With them, you can be vulnerable and safe and say what you really think. With them, you get to share your greatest joys as well as your deepest sorrows.

SUMMING IT UP

As you leave the campus, move to another city, take a new job, I would suggest to you the following priorities. The first thing that you need to do is to maintain your daily time with Christ. It is the life line of your fellowship with Him. You will get off track if you neglect the nourishment for this time with the Father.

Secondly, you need to begin to look for a church in which you feel comfortable. It should be one that boldly proclaims and teaches God's Word and one that allows you to be free to worship in the Spirit. It is hard to find a church that has a healthy balance of the Word and the Spirit, but try to find the one that does the best job of doing it.

Then, begin looking for a small group that fits your needs for this season of life. Finally, in the back of your mind continue to look for those to be in your Inner Circle. You may want to include your best friend from back on the campus even though he or she is now in another city. You can keep in touch by phone and email and maintain a close relationship. It will be very important to have this prayer support while you are making key decisions in your life. Also, get more connected with your parents and other family to be an emotional support base. By having each one of these four activities ongoing in your life, you will have an excellent chance of continuing to grow in your life with Christ. If you try to do it on your own and neglect these basic needs, you will have a very difficult time in keeping on the pathway of walking with Him.

Questions for Discussion:

1. How important have the small groups on the campus been in helping you to mature as a follower of Jesus?

2. What format of a small group has been most helpful for you over the years?

3. Do you have one or two close intimate fellow believers? How long did it take you to develop that relationship? Will you work to continue it after you leave the campus?

4. Is this type of intimacy easy for you, or do you struggle to really be vulnerable with another person?

CHAPTER 6
Gaining Wisdom, Finding a Mentor

"The things which you have heard from me in the presence of many witnesses, entrust these to faithful men who will be able to teach others also."

2 Timothy 2:2

"I still need help in making decisions and organizing my life. Now I'm responsible for managing everything in my life, and much of it is new. I struggle with getting enough sleep, exercising, and what to cook for dinner, especially since I don't have a car to go buy groceries, and I don't know how to cook."

Anna

Someone has said that the best things in life are free. That is certainly true when it comes to finding a mentor. I can tell you that, at 63 years of age, one of my greatest joys is to spend a lunch with a student or a young executive. What you may not realize is that leaders like me will share with you, at no charge, the life lessons that we have learned, while we may charge thousands of dollars to do that with a business client. We have usually had many failures and a few successes in our lives. We learn most from our failures. We are willing to share our life lessons with you so that you can mature faster, have an easier time we did, and accomplish more for the Kingdom of God. My friend, Dick Wynn, says that <u>mentors</u> help us with our values, morals, and character, which define us and give us direction and a foundation for our lives. Please understand that ALL true wisdom and insight come from God Himself. However, God uses His Word, the Holy Spirit, and other saints as spiritual mentors to impart His wisdom to us.

These mentors will be a key resource for you as you answer your question:

"In this time of your transition, how do you <u>obey</u> His command to make disciples and to <u>represent</u> and glorify Him, in order that many may believe?"

There are many examples of mentors in the Scriptures. Moses had Joshua, Elijah had Elisha, and Paul had Timothy. Who are the mentors that God has placed into your life? He or she could be a parent, a teacher, an uncle or aunt, a grandparent, a family friend, someone in a student ministry, a pastor, an older person in your church, or someone in your workplace. At this stage in life you need to be on the lookout for those that God is placing in your path to give a specific input into your life. The mentor may be one who is helping you in your spiritual life, your work life, your finances, or a hobby. They will give you practical wisdom that you cannot get in the classroom or get easily in books. They will be there to guide you and sit and answer questions for hours.

You can have different types of mentors. This person may be an <u>active</u> mentor that you meet with regularly. You could meet on a monthly basis for a cup of coffee or a meal together. You may do something fun together like go to a ball game, or go hunting or fishing, or to the mountains. The person could even be an <u>occasional</u> mentor who is available when you call upon them. This type of mentor can be a good source of information and counsel when you need help or advice in your career or job choices. This person could be a <u>passive</u> mentor from whom you learn from books or DVDs or speeches. They may not even be living, but you can still gain great insights from the lessons that they are passing on to you.

Where do you find these mentors? Well, you can start by looking in your church or the place where you are getting spiritual help. A great resource is to look at the leaders that relate to your campus ministry or come to your classes to speak. They may be key financial supporters, prayer warriors, or helpers in your campus ministry. Look for men and women who have a heart for God and are successful in their family, their career, and their service to the Body of Christ. These men and women are busy, and they will not want to waste their time. You may have to convince them that you are a serious follower of Christ and truly value their input. Your campus minister can probably give your fou or five names of leaders that they greatly respect. You can contact them and ask for an appointment for you to present your need and tell them your story.

Start now by deciding in which areas of your life you would like to get the wisdom from someone who has been there. Start keeping a list of questions that you would love to ask someone if you were given the opportunity. Begin observing the people around you. Look for the ones that seem to have weathered the storms of life, and are still on God's pathway. Someone once told me, "Never trust a leader who does not walk with a limp." Every mature leader will have gone through trials. You want to learn from them after they have gone through deep problems or suffering and have come out on the other side. We rarely learn from our successes, so learning from a leader who has everything going their way in their late 30's or early 40's may not be very valuable. I find that most leaders will experience some kind of deep trials in their 40's if not before. By the time that they are 50 years of age and certainly by 60, they will have many valuable life lessons to share.

These mentors may be helpful to you over a number of years or just for a season of life. I am not talking here about someone who is discipling you. That process is usually for a few months up to a year or two. Discipleship is normally helpful in getting you started in the basics of your Christian life. The discipling process helps you to become more like Christ. That could include learning to have a time with God, understanding how to study the Bible on your own, seeing various ways of sharing the Gospel with others, memorizing the Scriptures, managing your finances, being a responsible member of the local Body of believers, and being a better spouse or parent. The discipling process is very intense, usually requires weekly meetings, and is for a specific period of time and for specific areas of your life.

Coaching is another process that is very popular today in the business community. Coaching works primarily to develop our skills.   It is interesting to me that the secular world pays big bucks to coaches, and we in the Christian community are still hung up on large groups and do not use coaching as much as those who do not know Christ. Coaching is usually for a specific time and a specific project. It rarely lasts over a few weeks or months. Coaching usually requires a specialist who is an expert in a few areas or at least is an experienced coach and can take you through a very detailed process. The coach helps the person through the maze and holds them accountable. Coaching is usually short term while mentoring is usually a longer term relationship.

Discipleship, coaching, and mentoring are all about relationships. God wants you to be in relationships with others. The most important mentor in my life has been my Dad. Dad is now in his 80's and has Alzheimer's and does not even know my name today. But Dad has had a profound impact on my life. He modeled to me when I was a new believer at age nine that Christ can radically change a life. I saw my Dad spend time with Christ daily, and it changed his behavior. He changed as a father, a husband, a business leader, and a man.

A second mentor to me was a business leader named Gene. He took a group of young business leaders, including me, and put us into a small group that met every Saturday morning for years. Gene taught me how to study God's Word, how to communicate to others in a speaking situation, how to walk with God, and how to be a better man, husband, and father. Ford was another business leader who impacted my life as a mentor. He never spent much time with me; he lived in another state. However, I watched his life for many years and learned how he ministered in the workplace. He was a real estate professional who was constantly leading people to Christ, discipling other men, and modeling Christ's principles in everything that he did in business. These men greatly impacted my life, each in a different way.

When I was in my thirties, I made a list of the twelve men who had impacted my life up to that time. Each contributed something different. Some were active mentors, and others were occasional or passive mentors. Walt was a Bible teacher who taught me to think biblically, and Dr. David was a Bible teacher who gave me a love for the Scriptures. Charlie was a pastor who taught me to have fun and enjoy life, while Bob was a business leader who modeled to me that you could really minister to your customer and co-worker and share Christ in a non-religious way. Bob had discipled Ford some years before. Dr. Dave was my father-in-law who taught me how to love people and be a servant leader. He died at only 56 years of age, but had a profound impact on my life, his children, my children, and countless others in his medical profession. Dr. Hendricks is a seminary professor who has impacted my philosophy of life and ministry through his speaking and writing. Richard was my pastor who taught me humility and patience. Loren was the leader of a large ministry who modeled to me servant leadership and the simplicity of walking with Christ over a lifetime.Charlie worked for a large ministry and modeled to me the importance of investing your life into a few men. He discipled my Dad and Gene, and I would probably not be walking with Christ today without his investment into those two business leaders for 40 years. Most men are fortunate to have one mentor. God allowed me to have at least twelve of them before I was 40 years of age. I have a huge responsibility to make sure that these men got a good return on their investment into my life.

Let me close this chapter with one more story. Brian was active in a student ministry at a university near my home. When I speak to this group each year, I offer to have lunch with any student who wants to talk about integrating their faith and work. Brian took me up on the offer and brought a friend with him to lunch nearly 25 years ago. Each year or two after that he would call me for another lunch. He would ask me questions about our family business, because he was in one with his father. After about ten years, Brian asked me to read a book on mentoring and to mentor him. We met every two weeks. He would pick the topic, and I would seek to answer his questions. We did this for a year or so. Then, we both joined a monthly small group of business leaders. A few years later we each went through the sale of our long-term family businesses. Finally, about nine years ago, I asked Brian to be the CEO of a new business that I was starting. We had no sales for several years, lost a lot of money while waiting on an FDA approval, and learned many lessons from God. We have been business partners in several ventures and still have an occasional mentoring relationship. Brian is a tremendous leader, man of God, and has impacted many young men for Christ. He is a leader in our community. I have been blessed because Brian chose to ask me to spend some time with him. It has been one of the best things to ever happen to me. You need to offer someone that opportunity to be blessed by investing into your life and also learning from you.

Over the last 10 ro 20 years, God has brought a number of young men into my life that I have been able to actively or occasionally mentor. Many of the days that I am in my office in Oklahoma City, I go out to lunch with these young men. Some are entrepreneurs or business leaders. Others are students that are just heading out into the workplace. They call me every few months or once a year and tell me that it is time to meet again. Next to being with my three children and eight grandchildren, these are some of the most rewarding experiences of my life. I love to hear how God is working in their lives, teaching them new things. I love praying with them over the struggles that they are having, as I also share my own temptations, struggles, and challenges. They become wonderful encouragers and advisors to me; this is not just a one-sided relationship. I sincerely pray that you will experience the joy of being with a wise godly mentor who will help to steer you on the right path as you follow Christ!

Questions for Discussion:

1. Have you had a spiritual mentor in your life? What about a teacher or coach during your education?

2. How has one of your parents or key relatives been a mentor to you?

3. What characteristics will you look for in a mentor as you seek to find one in your career field or workplace?

4. If you could pick anyone in this nation to be a personal mentor to you, who would it be? Why? What are you going to do to find that kind of relationship?

CHAPTER 7
Coming Alive, Finding Your Passion

"For You formed my inward parts; You wove me in my mother's womb. I will give thanks to You, for I am fearfully and wonderfully made; Wonderful are Your works, and my soul knows it very well. My frame was not hidden from You, when I was made in secret, and skillfully wrought in the depths of the earth; Your eyes have seen my unformed substance; And in Your book were written all the days that were ordained for me, when as yet there was not one of them. How precious also are Your thoughts to me, O God! How vast is the sum of them!"

Psalms 139:13-17

"I wish I would have known your dreams would change. I wish I would have known that you are going to change and grow and that those dreams are going to change and grow with you. When you transition into your "twenty-somethings," your life is not going to turn out like you planned it – so go with it and don't freak out."

Lisa

The better you understand exactly how God has created you, the more effective you will be for Him. You are unique, and there is no one in all the earth that is exactly like you. God has made you as a special person so that He can use you for His glory. Who you are is determined by a number of different things. Your background, talents, interests, skills, education, personality, temperament, spiritual gifts, and experiences all have an impact on who you are and what you will become. These were not chosen by you or earned by you, but were given to you sovereignly in the providence of God. Therefore, your focus needs to be on Him and how He wants you to use what He has given you for His glory.

This brings us back again to that question:

"In this time of your transition, how do you <u>obey</u> His command to make disciples and to <u>represent</u> and glorify Him, in order that many may believe?"

Your parents, your family, and your **background** will have a huge impact on how you think and perceive the world. Your family and early life experience can be positive, or negative. May I encourage you to take the positive things and build on them. Do not dwell on the negative, but learn from those situations. Bible characters like Joseph and Daniel were able to overcome the difficult situations of their early years, and God will guide you to do the same.

All of us have various **talents**. I was never very athletic, but I am good at other types of games. We enjoy doing the things that we do well. So, try to spend time in your comfort zone. I was good at math and business, but not very good at history, science, and English literature. I could understand English grammar because it was a lot like math and made sense to me. Writing was difficult. I have learned to write with my wife's help and expertise and by doing a lot of it. So, sometimes you can develop a weak area by working on it. However, it will never be as easy as one in which you have natural talent. Try different things and take every opportunity that you can early in life. Know your talents and try to use them in your job and volunteer efforts. This will give you much more satisfaction in your life.

You need to work hard at developing your physical, mental, and social **skills**. For instance, public speaking is a skill that must be used and developed. I was initiated into speaking by joining the debate team in high school. At church, I developed this skill by teaching a Sunday school class and by speaking at retreats and conferences. I now get to do it all over the world, but that is because I have worked for years at developing the skill and using it frequently. I may still not be as smooth as a natural public speaker, but I speak with passion, using the Scriptures, and with many practical examples and stories. It takes a lot of time and years to develop our skills, but it is well worth the effort in both our careers and our leisure pursuits. So, focus on what you like to do and are good at doing. What things do others encourage you in doing? Do not compare yourself with others, but understand what you do well and really enjoy. While I was in my twenties, I compared myself with other young leaders and was very discouraged, because I was not very good at the things that they did so well. However, I had to realize that God had given me other gifts. I had to learn contentment in being the person that God had created me to be. This lesson in "comparison" was a huge stumbling block for me for several years, and I hope that you will not be taken off track by this deceitful habit.

Hopefully your **education** will be very helpful to you in your career. However, sometime it just provides for us the knowledge and skills to learn how to communicate and find the information that we need. Your education will in most cases open the door to opportunity, but then you must prove yourself by learning to adapt in your new environment and being productive for your employer or client. Your formal education will become less and less important as you go through your career. You need to be proud of your accomplishments in your education, but your co-workers will be more interested in how you perform and serve as part of the team, versus what degrees and awards you achieved in college. The education process helps us in determining what we enjoy and can do well, as well as those tasks and areas that we do not enjoy and consequently do not excel in them.

There are a multitude of **personality** tests, books, and courses that are available today. The DISC test is very popular in the business community. There is also the Myers-Briggs and countless others. The key is to find one or two that help describe you. The more comfortable you are with your uniqueness, the easier it will be for you to find your unique place on the team in the workplace, your family, your church, and your community. Your **temperament** is similar to your personality. I am a choleric by temperament. Knowing that helps me to relate to others that are totally different. I would suggest that you take some of the simple tests to understand both your personality and temperament. These will not change much as you age, so you may as well get comfortable with who you are and how God has created you.

SPIRITUAL GIFTS

Spiritual gifts are much more talked about today, and I hope that you have been able to take a short course in understanding the gifts that God has given to you as a child of God. Over recent years, there have been hundreds of books written in this area. The opinions are as diverse as the authors. Every follower of Christ has at least one spiritual gift. It is given to us when we are born again. Natural ability may indicate a spiritual gift, but the gift is different and given to produce eternal results, not temporal ones. These gifts are given to us as a result of God's grace and not our works. You can study spiritual gifts in three major passages: Romans 12, I Corinthians 12, and Ephesians 4.

Here is a partial list of spiritual gifts; administration, apostle, discernment, evangelism, exhortation, faith, giving, healing, helps, intercession, knowledge, leadership, mercy, miracles, missionary, pastor or shepherding, prophecy, service, teaching, tongues, and wisdom. Some would add a number of gifts to this list, while others would debate the validity of some of the gifts today. There are many helpful websites that not only give information but allow you to take a test. Most of them are free. These are constantly changing and being updated, so please do your own search. The following are the best ones that I have discovered:

www.kodachrome.org	www.churchgrowth.org
www.buildingchurch.com	www.christianet.com
www.elmertowns.com	www.spreadinglight.com
www.spiritualgiftstest.com	

Let me share with you a couple of illustrations. You are like an electric ice cream freezer, in which God prepares a unique flavor of ice cream to be enjoyed by others. You are most useful when you are empty and clean. Then you will be turned and churned to produce the best ice cream. It is best when done correctly by plugging into the power source of the Holy Spirit. Many believers are still trying to produce something out of their own efforts with an old hand crank. After people taste the ice cream, the preparer (God) gets the credit, not the freezer itself. We are just an instrument that God uses to feed others.

You are also like a race car driver. The cars come in all different models and styles and colors. The drivers are from different nations and are every color and size. But, the master engine builder (God the Father) has built a special engine (your spiritual gift) just for you. The tires provide traction, and the blisters can lead to blowouts and crashes. The tires represent God's Word, keeping us on the track. Without constant renewal, we will crash. Blisters on the tires represent sin in our lives. Without repentance, we will have a blowout. Without the fuel of the Holy Spirit and His filling, we will not complete the race. All of us need frequent pit stops of time with Him. We must be in constant radio contact with the "spotter" (represents other believers who warn us of danger) and listen to the communication from our "crew chief", Jesus Christ, who makes the decisions and tells us exactly what to do.

As you learn about yourself by spending time with God, time with those who know you best, and studying each of these areas, you will be much more comfortable in the way the Creator of the universe has made you to be an instrument of service to Him. Remember, we, as the instruments, are like the violin that is in the Master's hand. The focus is not to be on the violin, but on the Master, Himself. He knows us well and understands exactly how to get the right music out of our lives. The key is for us to continually <u>surrender</u> ourselves totally to Him. We must put ourselves back on the altar to be used by Him. We tend to keep "jumping off" and trying to do our own thing instead of making ourselves completely available to Him. As you think about gifts and talents, remember that it is more about "who we are" rather that "what we do". It is more about "being" (our John 15 relationship with Christ) than "doing". "Relationship" should be the focus, not the "activity".

If we keep our <u>relationship with Him</u> and <u>who we are becoming</u> in Christ on track, then what we "do" and our "activities" will naturally glorify Him. So, just keep these warnings in perspective. We really need to know ourselves, but the key to knowing ourselves is to focus on KNOWING CHRIST. That is why daily intimacy with Him will be important for the rest of your life. Believe me, it is exciting but is a challenge to keep in focus.

Questions for Discussion:

1. Share with the group how your family, your lifestyle growing up, and your hometown have influenced you to this point in your life.

2. What are two or three of the talents that God gave to you at birth that you have developed?

3. Could you share with us your basic personality or temperament?

4. Have you discovered one or more of your spiritual gifts?

CHAPTER 8

Dollars and Sense, Financing Your Dream

> *"Give, and it will be given to you. They will pour into your lap a good measure — pressed down, shaken together, and running over. For by your standard of measure it will be measured to you in return."*

Luke 6:38

> *"The rich rules over the poor, And the borrower becomes the lender's slave."*

Proverbs 22:7

"I think a huge transition I faced was financially figuring out how to be an adult. As much as life prepares you for it, it is just overwhelming at times, and it's hard, it's really hard."

Lisa

Many university students today are graduating with $40,000 to $50,000 of debt from student loans. Those who are going to graduate school, medical school, or law school may run up debt of well over $100,000. This is causing tremendous stress on the marriages and the financial situations of these young adults. In addition to this, many graduates have two or three credit cards with balances and a card payment. Let me explain it to you in very simple language. If you have these kinds of debts, then you are in bondage to the lender. You will never have financial freedom if you are putting such a large percentage of your pay check towards paying the interest expense of the principal payments of such debt.

These sobering facts tie in directly with our objective:

"In this time of your transition, how do you <u>obey</u> His command to make disciples and to <u>represent</u> and glorify Him, in order that many may believe?"

YOU will <u>not</u> have the freedom to follow and obey Him if you are a slave to your accumulated debt. One long-time campus minister tells me that such debt is a major roadblock for students who wanted to be available to be used by God, but were unaware of the steep consequences of such debt. And recent surveys show us that these loans, that were not even available just a few decades ago, have now trapped many of our current graduates. Here are the latest figures:

College Students with student debt in 2008: **

Private for profit universities	96%
Private non-profit	72%
Public colleges/universities	67%

It is probable that you have some student loans. This is just ONE of the financial issues that you will now be facing. You may have thought that when you left the campus and got a good paying job, your financial problems would be over. However, the opposite is true. Your income will go up dramatically for most of you, but your expenses will also increase. The norm is that TOTAL debt increases during your first few years out of college as you maximize multiple CREDIT CARDS, buy a "deserved" new car, furnish your new apartment or house, and buy those clothes that you NEED for your new job.

The first step to financial freedom is to have a PLAN. I recommend that you enroll in one of the many good classes that are available at your church or in your community. The best one that I have found is the *Crown Financial Ministries* small group study, which is available in many churches. It is a ten-week, life changing course. If your church does not have it, go to the web at www.crown.org and find a class near you. Crown has many books, seminars, and resources available to help you to achieve financial freedom. Be sure to get a copy of the *Money Map*. If Crown is not available in your area, then you may want to check out www.DaveRamsey.com, which has many helpful resources. This is a for-profit organization, but his teaching is based on Biblical principles. He presents his ***Financial Peace University*** in many cities across the USA.

Now let me share with you a few general principles that will help you get on the pathway to financial freedom.

- The first thing to remember is that **work** was created by God, not as a curse, but for our benefit to bless us and those around us. He wants us to care for His creation, and we are to be stewards of the resources that He has placed under our care. We do not "own" anything, but are simply caretakers of the possessions that He places in our hands for a short time. So, work is important to God. We should enjoy our work and use the talents and gifts that He has given us to bless others.

- As we earn money, we need to handle it in a biblical manner. The first rule is that we need to **spend less than we make** and have a **margin**. The average American is spending slightly more than they make each year and gradually accumulating a large amount of debt. When you get your first pay check, it will look like you have a lot of extra money to spend. You need to be careful that you are having enough payroll taxes deducted, so that you do not get into trouble at the end of the year when paying income taxes. Particularly if you are single, without the interest expense of a home loan and other deductions, you need to make sure that you allow enough for income taxes.

- The first thing that we do after we get our check is to **give to God** to acknowledge his provision for our lives. Paul tells us in 2 Corinthians 9:7, *"Each one must do just as he has purposed in his heart, not grudgingly or under compulsion, for God loves a cheerful giver."* The Old Testament gives us the tithe of 10% as a standard for giving. I believe that is a good place to start, but as stewards, we must realize that God owns it all, and that He may want us to give much more than that. We should give regularly, proportionately, not out of fear or self justification, but cheerfully (1 Corinthians 16, Luke 18, and 2 Corinthians 8). We should give voluntarily, generously, secretly, and sacrificially (II Corinthians 8 and 9, Matthew 6 and 12). We should give to the widows, orphans, poor, and aliens (Deuteronomy 14). We should give to those who have helped us spiritually (Matthew 10 and Galatians 6). We should give to those in the Body of Christ who are experiencing hard times, to those who have never heard the Gospel, and to organizations which will produce the best return on our investment of God's money (Acts 11, Matthew 28, and 2 Timothy 2). Once you get your sight on God and His agenda instead of your wants, then you will begin to have financial freedom and learn the joy of giving for His purposes.

- After taking care of your giving, the next thing you need to do is to set aside a small fund for **emergencies**. This keeps you from having a crisis and having to pay too much to fix the problem. If you do not buy that new car and still have that "old" one from college, then allow some margin and set aside money for repairs. If you decide to buy that older house instead of renting, then you will really need to set aside funds for repairs that you never imagined. You will need to get medical insurance. Do not think that you will remain healthy just because you are young. You will probably have a large deductible, so any unexpected physician visits or prescriptions will have to come out of your pocket. Then there are those unexpected trips back home to see a sick family member or attend a best friend's wedding. All of these seem to catch us unaware, and you need to allow for them in your new emergency fund. It takes all the stress out of your finances and trains you not to rely on the new credit card. You sure do not want to call the parents, because you are now "independent" and learning all the joys of being responsible for your own finances.

- Next, develop a **budget** plan for your spending; there are many different ways and systems to do that (Proverbs 16:9). As you set up your apartment or first house, do not spend a lot on furniture. Do not get into debt buying things that you cannot afford, because this leads to slavery (Proverbs 22:7). Go to garage sales and check with family and friends. You can make do with less. Have a plan to pay off your debt as soon as possible, and start by paying off the high interest credit cards while working down the debt on your student loans, if any, and by lowering your car payment. You will learn that you can buy a good used car that is only a few years old, with cash that you have set aside, and save a lot in interest and principal. Or you can save more and buy a new car and drive it for many years. I can afford to drive a new car, but I drive a good seven-year-old car which meets my needs. This allows me to spend more money on my family and things for His kingdom.

- Until you get rid of your expensive high interest debt, you will experience the frustration of financial pressure and stress. After you have attacked the credit card debt, the car loans, the student loans, and the other consumer debt, you can really begin to **save**. You can save for that emergency fund, a vacation, the new car, the down payment of a home, the retirement plan, and the education fund for your children. Be sure to maximize the benefit of your employer contributing to your retirement plan. Most 401-K employer plans match 25%, or 50%, or 100%, and you should take advantage of that. Your home can be one of the best investments that you make. It also gives a sense of security to your spouse and your financial future.

Let me give you one last tip. The biggest problem area in a marriage is not sex. It is the financial area. More marriages break up because of stress in this area than any other issue. The best way to help your marriage is to have clear communication about finances, and decide which partner is responsible for what things. Clearly go over the plan for giving, the list of debts, the budget, the spending plan, and the saving priorities. Having a plan and peace in the area of finances will be the best way to improve your marriage relationship. As we seek God first in the financial area, He will help us get all of our priorities in place (Matthew 6:33)

**USA Today, page B-1, August 14th, 2009

Questions for Discussion:

1. Do you have some student loans? What is your plan for paying them off? How many credit cards do you currently have? Do you pay off the balance each month? What precautions are you taking to make sure that you do not get into credit card bondage?

2. What does it mean to live with margin? Have you calculated what percentage that the various payroll taxes will take out of your "gross" income?

3. What percentage of your income have you been giving to God during your college years? Will you be supporting the campus ministry or Christian college that you attended with some of your giving funds?

4. Do you currently have a budget or a financial plan of any kind? If not, when will you make one? Who will hold you accountable? Are finances a stressful area for you now? Will you attend a financial small group or workshop in order to make this area a priority for your new life?

CHAPTER 9
Life is Brief, Get Started Right

"LORD, remind me how brief my time on earth will be. Remind me that my days are numbered, and that my life is fleeing away. My life is no longer than the width of my hand. An entire lifetime is just a moment to you; human existence is but a breath. We are merely moving shadows, and all our busy rushing ends in nothing. We heap up wealth for someone else to spend. And so, Lord, where do I put my hope? My only hope is in you."

Psalms 39:4-7 (NLT)

"Finding the right girl is really hard, but being the right kind of guy is even harder. I am still learning to live abandoned to God and His will."

Evan

In this closing chapter, I want to briefly mention a few things about your health, your habits, and your family. We need to remember that life is brief, and we do not know how long we will live. My sister died at 39 years of age, yet my grandmother lived until 105. Several years ago, I was told that I had a rare disease. Only 75% of the patients lived for five years. I suddenly realized the brevity of life and that I might not live my 70 years. It caused me to re-evaluate my lifestyle and goals. After the disease had been in remission for ten years, I am dealing with it again. I now want to live every day to the fullest, so that I can maximize my time on this earth to glorify Him. Regardless of age, each of use needs to live with an eternal perspective. So, we should form good habits while we are young. The experts say that it takes us three to seven weeks to form a habit, so we need to be diligent about forming good habits in our health, spiritual lives, social life, and finances.

"In this time of your transition, how do you obey His command to make disciples and to represent and glorify Him, in order that many may believe?"

By forming good habits now, you will be able to more readily glorify Him in your sphere of influence. It will be much easier for you to be sensitive to His Spirit in various areas of your life, instead of responding to the flesh. You will be able to disciple others in the disciplines that you have applied to your own life.

As a young adult, you can have bad eating habits now and still get away with it. However, that will not last long. So start now with a regular exercise program three or four days a week. I was in my mid 30's before I established good habits in exercise, and it takes a long time to catch up. Find physical activities that you enjoy and can do with others. Get a gym membership and exercise regularly. Find a friend and walk or jog together. You will feel better and think more clearly. It has taken me another 20 or more years to establish good eating habits. Eat healthy, and it will save you many medical issues later in life. Learn to make good choices when eating out or at home alone. Have others hold you accountable if that is needed. Do not be addicted to anything, particularly alcohol, drugs, or tobacco. First of all, these will hurt your testimony. Next they will damage your health, and they are very expensive financially. Be careful about becoming a slave to anything.

Be cautious about what books you read, movies and tv that you watch, and music that you listen to. These things influence our thinking and our actions. We become like the things that we put into our minds. We become like the friends with whom we spend time. We eventually do the things that we think about. And we think about the things that our heart is set on. So, above all else guard your heart and your mind (Proverbs 4:23). We must concentrate on getting positive input into our minds. You are in transition and at an age that you are very susceptible to your passions and emotions. Be a Joseph, Daniel, or an Esther. Form good habits each day and have a good group of friends that love Jesus and want to live for Him.

There is a great passage on priorities in Ephesians 5:15-17 (J. B. Philips, 1960), *"Live life, then, with a due sense of responsibility, not as men who do not know the meaning and purpose of life but as those who do. Make the best use of your time, despite all the difficulties of these days. Don't be vague but firmly grasp what you know to be the will of the Lord."* Learn to schedule your time well and have time for the most important things. Build freedom into your schedule for leisure, for rest, and for friends and family. Your schedule will be tighter than it was in school, and you will have to be much more organized. However, you will adapt and do well if you get the most important things done on time. Work on choosing the BEST and not just the good. A favorite verse for me has been Psalm 25:12-14 (TLB), *"Where is the man who fears the Lord? God will teach him how to choose the best. He shall live within God's circle of blessing and his children shall inherit the earth. Friendship with God is reserved for those who reverence Him, with them alone He shares the secrets of His promises."* If you seek God first, then He will help you choose His very best plans for you each day.

Finally, let me say a few words about your family. The older you get, the more important your immediate family and extended family will become. Make it a priority to get time with them and do whatever it costs to travel to see them. Many of you are single at the moment. Some of you will remain single. However, the majority of you will eventually get married. As you date and choose a spouse, try to help them fit into your larger family. I should mention that if you remain single, your immediate family of origin will be even MORE important as you progress through life. My wife and I have a great relationship with our children, with their spouses, and even with their parents. Your relationship with your family can make your life either bitter, or better. You need to really work on building bridges of relationships. Even bad situations can be greatly helped through prayer and a lot of hard work. Go through reconciliation if needed, but try to keep the relationships open and working.

If you are close to being married, understand that next to your walk with Christ, the most important thing in your life will be your spouse. God wants this relationship to be fulfilling for both of you. Divorce will complicate your life and give you pain for the rest of it. So, do everything that you can to get with the right person and stay with them, whatever it takes. Marriage is hard work. Davidene and I are in our 43rd year. We have three children, their spouses, and eight grandchildren. All of these relationships take work, but the rewards are well worth it. So, it is MUCH BETTER to remain single than to rush into the wrong marriage.

Right now make a list of what characteristics you want in a spouse. Begin to pray and ask God for that person for your life. Do not be afraid to reach high and believe God for the very best. Do not even date someone that you would not want to marry. Look for a mate that has a heart for God and complements you in every way. I married way above my head, to a woman who is smart, beautiful, talented, and godly. It is possible for you to do the same. Davidene is a great mother and was the *Mother of the Year* for Oklahoma a few years ago. She is a teacher, mentor, writer, a dare devil in sports activities, counselor, speaker, leader, and friend. You can have that kind of spouse. Really, marriage is about serving and trying to get over our selfishness.

If you are still single, enjoy this special time. I have some wonderful friends who have been life long-singles. They have been used wonderfully in the Kingdom of God and, just like Paul, have had a capacity for friendships, ministry, and service to others that we married folks just have not had the capacity to accomplish. But, whether you remain single or not, you really need to work on the area of purity. This area will influence you for the rest of your life. Realize that every action has consequences and ask God to give you strength every day. Even if you get married, those bad habits will creep into your life. So, deal with them at arm's length, be ruthless with your physical desires, and God will reward you just as He did Joseph and others. Again, get your peers to help you to stay pure in this area. The small victories that you have will pay huge dividends in the future.

IF and when you get married, work hard to have a few couples with which you can learn together. These were some great times in our early marriage. We were still in school and working and did not have much. But, the fellowship with these couples was marvelous. Look for an older couple at your church who will take you under their wings and mentor you. They will be a valuable resource to you for wisdom, counsel, and as a role model. They will help you over the rough spots in the road during those first few years. Your marriage will show you how much work there is to do still in your life and walk with God. However, God is a God of grace, and, hopefully, you and your spouse will strive to give the same grace to each other. The key is to continue to pursue God and allow Him to work on our lives to mold us into the kind of person that He can use. If we are patient and obedient, then we will eventually see the light and be encouraged that we can make it. Life is a journey, and we must persevere and stay on His pathway.

In conclusion, your physical life, your single life or marriage, your mental input, your family, and your priorities will each have a huge impact on how you transition through this phase of your life. Remember that God has a perfect plan for your life, and your responsibility is to listen to Him and follow Him in each area of your life. He wants the best for you and is preparing you to be useful for Him for years to come. Our prayer is that you will be used by God to impact the lives of many in your sphere of influence.

Questions for Discussion:

1. What are you doing daily to insure an eternal perspective for your life?

2. What are the habits that you struggle with as you seek to be healthy physically, spiritually, and socially?

3. What are you putting into your mind regularly through the internet, books, TV, movies, music, or other means, that is not edifying or glorifying to Christ? Who is holding you accountable?

4. What are your priorities? Do you have trouble in saying NO to the good in order to do the best? Is your family a priority, and are those relationships being cared for or ignored?

CHAPTER 10

HAVE YOU EVER SEEN A SECULAR COLOR?
A Word for College Students Transitioning to the Work World

by Christian Overman

As you transition from college life to your career, I encourage you to keep Psalm 24:1 in mind: "*The earth is the Lord's and all it contains, the world and those who dwell in it.[1]*"

If you think you are headed for a "secular" job in a "secular" world, I have news for you. There are *no secular jobs* out there, because there is *no secular world!*

Allow me to explain.

No matter which career path you may take, whether you make your mark in business, politics, the arts or homemaking, you will always be working in the Lord's field. This is because there is no other place to work! It is all His turf. From the plastic of your computer keyboard, to the rubber tires on your automobile, it all belongs to Him. The earth is the Lord's and *all it contains.*

Not only does the earth and all it contains belong to the Lord, but He is also continuously sustaining it through time. *"All things have been created through Him and for Him...and in Him all things hold together"* (Col. 1:16-17). Without Christ actively holding all things together, your computer would evaporate, and the wheels of your car would disintegrate.

And that's not all. Acts 10:36 tells us: "Jesus is *Lord* of all." So in what place can we work where Jesus is not Lord? It is true that many people we work

---

1 All Scripture references in this chapter are from the New American Standard Bible.

with may not *recognize* Him as Lord, but this does not negate the fact that Jesus *is* Lord. He is Lord of *all*, whether the company we work for acknowledges Him as such or not! The Lord is "head over all" (I Chronicles 29:11). No matter where we work, the ultimate authority is Christ. In the years to come, you may work in many places that ignore the Lordship of Christ, and in some places that actively deny it, but you will never work in any place that is exempt from it.

I once looked up the word "secular" in a dictionary, back in the days when people flipped through paper pages. It said the word "secular" meant "not related to religion." I think this is how most people would interpret the word "secular." And when I looked up the word "religion" in the same dictionary, it said: "a system of beliefs centering on a supernatural being." So if we put the two definitions together, the definition of "secular" reads something like this: "not related to a system of beliefs centering on a supernatural being."

But is there any aspect of creation that is not related to Christ? Is there any place that lies outside the realm of God's affairs? Is there any sphere of life's activity that exists independently of God, on its own, in a vacuum, somehow separated from His ownership, interest and involvement? Where exactly *is* the "secular" world, anyway?

You may go to work in a "secular*ized*" field, where God is ignored and never mentioned, except as a swear word. Yes, we do live in a "secular*ized*" world, in which the Lord is not often taken seriously. Yes, you may have experienced a secular*ized* education for the past seventeen years, but you will never have a truly "secular" job, because there truly is no "secular" world.

DISMANTLING DUALISM

Dualism is the idea that life can be divided into two distinct compartments, with a wide gap between. Dualism divorces public lives from private lives. It divorces the corporate world from the personal world. It divorces the material world from the spiritual world. It divorces the body from the soul. It divorces the "secular" from the sacred.

This is nonsense. According to the biblical worldview, there is only one Jesus who is the Creator, Sustainer and Lord of all. He ties it all together. We should not try to break it apart. We cannot. We may *think* we can (and this is the problem), but we cannot.

The Word of God applies the same to our work life as to our personal life. It is an eternal presence that transcends all time and space. It abides forever. It speaks to every task you will ever engage in, whether on the job or off. It casts light on every appointment you will ever make, and every sale you will close. God's Word is not just a Sunday thing. It is a Monday thing, too: all day, and all week long.

Nothing has had a more debilitating effect upon the ability of followers of Christ to integrate their faith with their everyday work than Western dualism has. It is insidious. I encourage you to dismantle any hold it may have upon your mind.

How? By replacing Western dualism with a different paradigm. A biblical paradigm that will allow you to see the world, including your work, through the lens of a much different window. It is a way of seeing that's as old as the ancient Hebrews. A way of seeing that was normal for David, Deborah, and Daniel. But for most of us to get there, it involves a significant shift in thought.

The roots of Western dualism go back to ancient Greece. Plato had the idea that since everything in the physical world deteriorates and eventually turns to dust, the material world must not have any real value or significance. He thought the only things that had true value were the things that were eternal and incorruptible. The eternal things he turned to were *ideals of the mind.* Ideals that never change or decay, but last forever, like ideal beauty, ideal truth, and ideal justice.

In the process of elevating such ideals, he devalued physical matter. He practiced a form of trancelike meditation to escape from the physical world. He viewed the physical body as "the prison house of the soul." For Plato, the physical, material world was a mere "shadow" of the "real" world that lay above and beyond. Plato lived in a culture that did not have a high regard for manual labor. It was beneath the dignity of a citizen of Athens.

A biblical view of work, however, is much different. In the beginning, God created all physical matter, and He said: *"It is good."* The First Commission given by God to humanity was to steward and govern over the material world He created (Gen. 1:26-28). God instructed Adam to "tend and keep" the garden. This was indeed work, and this work was not a curse. The curse came later, at the entrance of sin into the world. That curse made our work more difficult, for sure, but work itself was never a curse.

The ancient Hebrews saw the material world quite differently than the Greeks. All of creation was celebrated as God's good handiwork (see Psalm 19). And humans were given the responsible role of managing God's creation (see Psalm 8), which requires all kinds of work. "Earth-tending" is a very big job.

In Jesus' day, the rabbis were expected to not only know Torah (the Law), but to be skilled at a physical trade. Paul was a tentmaker. Other well-known rabbis of his day were woodworkers. It was thought that a Jewish father who did not teach his son the law and a trade would cause him to be a fool and a thief.

Plato's dualistic way of thinking was like a London double-decker bus. In the "higher" level were the eternal ideals. In the "lower" level was temporal matter. Over centuries, Plato's philosophy gained popularity among the thinkers of the ancient world. Some of these thinkers became Christian leaders in the first centuries of the church, and these leaders mixed Platonic ideas with Christianity. The eventual result was the division of work into "higher" and "lower" occupations. So today, "sacred" occupations have to do with "higher" things, like pastoring, preaching, evangelizing, and singing worship songs on Sunday morning. "Secular" occupations have to do with "lower" things, like selling real estate, manufacturing airplanes, and designing software in the Monday-through-Friday work world. So, in *this* world, work for the Christian is second rate: less important, common and of lower value. We have forgotten there is only one world, and it is all God's world.

HEAVEN IS NOT YOUR HOME—YET

Many evangelical Christians have sung that old chorus, "this world is not my home, I'm just a-passing through" so many times they have come to believe it. The fact is, for now, this world *is* our home, and Christ instructs us to occupy it until He comes again! This act of occupation takes place in every endeavor of humanity. And while we are not to be *of* the world, God fully intends for us to be *in* the world.

The sinister "sacred-secular split" has subtly given many Christians "permission" to leave their Christianity outside the workplace door. As a consequence, the world can't always distinguish Christians from non-Christians in the work world. But you can change this!

You may not know exactly what line of work your occupation will involve, whether medicine or music, but know this: work in this temporal world is a good thing. It is a God thing. That's because it is God's world, and the physical realm, although temporal, is all God's "stuff." (Remember Psalm 24:1.) God intends for us to rule over His stuff well. This is the great joy of work. A joy that can be realized by those who embrace God's *First* Commission found in Genesis 1:26-28: to rule over all the earth.

This understanding of work is not common today. Followers of Christ in the work-world have had the rug pulled out from under them by a false dualism that leads them to think "the Lord's work" is something done only by pastors and missionaries, or by volunteers on the weekend. We have reduced the Great Commission of Matthew 28:18-20 to the task of saving souls. While saving souls is critical, and it is implicit in Christ's Great Commission, it is not the whole of His last command.

The Great Commission is not only a command to baptize new believers, but to make disciples of all nations. A big part of Christ's Great Commission, as He said, is *"teaching them to observe all that I have commanded you."* Where are these new disciples going to observe all that Christ commanded? Just in heaven? Hardly. Jesus had the here-and-now in mind.

Christ's Great Commission is fulfilled as His followers observe all that He commanded within the realm of business, government, the arts, media, education, and every other sphere of human endeavor on the planet. The degree of corruption we often find in these spheres today may be because Christ-followers have either opted out of them, or we have never realized that we are supposed to observe all that Christ commanded within the context of these kinds of jobs. We have all been duped by dualism.

It is in the work world where we have a prime opportunity to observe all that Christ commanded us. What better place to put our faith to work in the world than in our everyday workplaces? Serve God, serve people. Love God, love people. You can do this through almost any profession. And get paid for it, to boot!

Yes, God calls some people to be pastor-preachers. Thank God for John Wesley! If you are called to this kind of work, go for it! But God also calls people like William Wilberforce, the 18th Century member of British Parliament who labored twenty years to abolish slavery and reform British culture.

As a young convert, Wilberforce thought about quitting his work in Parliament so he could go into "the ministry." But his friend John Newton, a former slave trader who wrote the words to the hymn, "Amazing Grace," encouraged Wilberforce to remain in Parliament. The world can thank Newton for his good advice, and for Wilberforce's commitment to apply his discipleship to his work in the public square. This is where he did his most effective work, "salting" and "lighting" the world through his everyday job as a politician.

A good way to start your transition from the world of academia to the world of work is to realize there is no sacred-secular divide, and that God has a divine purpose for your everyday work in this temporal, material world. I hope this realization will inspire you to seek Christ's Kingdom first, and to apply the precepts of His Kingdom in various workplaces of the material world, through all the days of your life.

May you seek His Kingdom through Scripture, through prayer, and through learning from others who have traveled your way before. My prayer for you is that a great enthusiasm for a work-life of purpose and significance *in this present world*, through whatever work you do, will never be squelched.

May your everyday work be used to fulfill Christ's prayer that His Father's will be done *on earth* as it is in heaven. This is what He has in mind for you, and for your work.

Questions for Discussion:

1. What causes us to separate the "secular" and the "spiritual"?

2. Give an example of how Jesus showed that "temporal" is important.

3. Why do we view the "professionals" as more "spiritual" than the rest of us?

4. What can you do to remind yourself that your daily work is really a "high calling"?

Christian Overman, D. Min, M. Ed.
Founding Director, Worldview Matters

Blog: www.biblicalworldviewmatters.blogspot.com

Web: www.worldviewmatters.com

Dr. Christian Overman is the Founding Director of *Worldview Matters,* www.biblicalworldview.com, and the author of *Assumptions That Affect Our Lives, God's Pleasure At Work,* and *The Difference One Life Can Make.* He has spoken on the topic of biblical worldview and the intersection of faith and work across North America, as well as in Central America, Europe, Africa and Asia. Christian and his wife, Kathy, have four adult children and ten grandchildren. They reside near Seattle, Washington.

CHAPTER 11

Bridging The Secular and Sacred Divide:

Living Out A Holistic Worldview

by Jeremy Story

The Problem

Recently a New York City college student told me about a problem he was having with the pastor of a church he was attending. "I am a music business major, and I want to go into the music industry to produce albums. My pastor and my parents think I shouldn't do that." "Why?", I asked, thinking his parents and pastor were concerned about the difficulty getting a job in such an exclusive industry. "They tell me that the music industry is full of dishonest and immoral people. They are concerned I will become like them," he replied.

I hear a thought process like this one about the 'secular world' most every week. When I studied law in college, people told me not to become a lawyer because, "Lawyers are dishonest." It is as if certain fields or parts of our society are off limits to God and his people. To hear many, you would think some places are beyond the reign and reach of Christ.

The Merriam-Webster Online Dictionary defines 'secular' as "not overtly or specifically religious" or "not ecclesiastical or clerical." It is hard to define 'secular' apart from an understanding of the word 'sacred.' Most dictionaries define 'sacred' as the opposite of secular, meaning "set apart for religion or God."

This isn't a fully biblical worldview. Dividing the world into things which are more spiritual and less spiritual often leads us into a path of dualistic thought that Jesus fought against. As followers of Jesus we must live with a holistic worldview which seeks to bring all areas of society into submission under Christ. This dualistic thought pattern lurks beneath the way many believers think about church leadership (clergy v. laity) and evangelistic mission (believers v. the world). Discarding this dualistic mindset and pursuing a holistic Christian worldview is a critical factor in successfully transitioning out of college with a thriving faith in Jesus Christ.

When students fail to transition, we blame it on bad campus ministry, moral failure in that graduate's life, or inability to connect into a 'real' church as opposed to a parachurch group. While these problems may be contributing factors, the real cause is much deeper. Those of us in church or parachurch campus ministry leadership discuss the bruise on top of the patient's skin while life-threatening internal bleeding proceeds underneath. Meanwhile, we wonder why many of our patients keep dropping dead with mild bruises.

The History of The Problem

This dualistic juxtaposition among Christians, of the more and less spiritual or the secular and sacred worlds, is as old as the New Testament. Christianity was initially called "The Way." It was a primarily Jewish sect that professed Jesus to be resurrected and God incarnate. As more and more Gentiles became Christians, they brought with them the Greek mindset. Prevalent among the Greeks was a dualistic way of thinking about the physical and spiritual worlds which divided them away from each other. Later, this led to the Gnostic movement which was declared a heresy by the mainstream church.

Paul writes against the origins of this stream of thought in Corinthians. In 1 Corinthians 15 Paul refutes those within the 'Christian' stream who argued there was no resurrection from the dead. How could those who claimed to be Christian come to deny the resurrection? They started with the seemingly innocent premise of dividing the world into the spiritual and unspiritual.

Notice how Paul refutes this premise in 1 Corinthians 15. He affirms a physical resurrection. He denotes a difference between the physical and spiritual realm but doesn't claim they are mutually exclusive. Instead he explains how God will redeem that which is broken and give us new physical bodies that will be imperishable and rebuilt in a way we can hardly imagine now.

This is an important distinction. The Bible often describes how the secular world and the flesh are at war with the kingdom of God. However, it never abandons the concept that God is about redeeming that secular world, invading it, dominating it, and reforming it in His image. The Bible advocates a "both/and" theology rather than an "either/or" theology.

Breaking The Cycle

How does this apply to your life and to transition out of college? Students take one or more of these steps within five or so years of graduation: they get a job, get married, have kids, and/or build their careers. While in college many students have a great experience pursuing God in a thriving Christ-centered community of their peers through their parachurch or church-based college ministry.

Suddenly in their job, this same experience of a huddle of believers is missing. Many students subliminally and quietly conclude that God must not be applicable or active in the workplace or 'secular' world. As they encounter difficulties in marriage or in raising kids, they also quietly conclude God must not be applicable there either. In a subtle and incremental way, they conclude the relationship with God they had in college is not transferable to the real 'secular' world. It is not a far leap from there to conclude that God must not be real at all since He only seems to thrive in 'sacred' arenas.

God is left as a fond distant memory of the days when they were naive and things were easier. Soon we hear of Bill or Sue who was an 'on-fire' leader in college but, who now doesn't believe God exists. This process begins by dividing God away from parts of your life you deem as unspiritual or secular activities.

God wants to own all of you, he also wants to use you to extend His kingdom and experience His reign everywhere you go and in everything you do. This applies equally to washing the dishes, reading the Bible, socializing with co-workers, praying, designing computers, or managing a business.

A Holistic View of Your Spiritual Authority And Access To God

Let's look at some direct implications of thinking holistically about our relationship with God. Are you aware that you are a priest? You have access to the same power and spiritual authority as does the most Godly and influential pastor you know.

Ephesians 4 reminds us that leaders in the church were set apart to lead others to be full priests rather than to take over the entire realm of ministry or to dictate the 'vision' for particular ministry direction to the masses. The church is to be equipped by leaders who are equally spiritual as everyone else rather than people who are set apart as extra-spiritual.

Jesus, rather than one central human figure, is to be the Head of the church and through the Holy Spirit, God can equally confirm in the hearts of a group of leaders seeking Him, clear direction for the future. Likewise, all Christians can equally hear the Holy Spirit guiding, empowering them how to 'pastor' their workplaces and do not need a 'Pastor' telling them when and how they can minister.

We all benefit from pastors and other leaders who are not spiritual specialists but fellow co-laborers who can coach and encourage us as we minister in our own field of influence. In one model, a select few people own origins of "The Vision" and "The Ministry." In the other model, every believer owns the origins of Christ's vision and ministry.

Indeed the very death and resurrection of Jesus affirms a holistic view of leadership and the literal and practical priesthood of every believer. The Jerusalem temple at the time of Jesus was divided into four courts or areas. The Western entrance was the Court of Gentiles where everyone could walk. The next court was the Court of Women into which specifically Jewish women could walk. If you were a Jewish male, you could walk closer to the center of the temple into the Court of Israel. Lastly, if you were a Jewish priest, you could enter the Court of Priests. The center of the temple mount hosted the Holy of Holies where God's presence dwelled. Its entrance was covered with a large ornate curtain.

When Jesus died, Matthew writes, *"At that moment, the curtain of the temple was torn in two from top to bottom. The earth shook and the rocks split.* (Matt 27:51)"* This was no random occurrence. God was making the statement that Jesus' death and soon-coming resurrection was obliterating the walls and gates between the courts.

Under the Old Covenant, your access to the presence of God depended on who you were. Under the New Covenant, everyone has equal access to the very presence and power of God. The New Testament takes it a step further to show that believers are the Temple God. The Holy Spirit now dwells inside us.

Any theology that concludes there is some special part of God, which is only available to a special higher spiritual class of Christians, is dualistic, and is in opposition to the basic principles of the New Testament.

This means you are the priest and kingdom bringer of your workplace. You have full authority to establish the church within the field that you work. You can share Christ with Heavenly authority with the most lost souls, disciple your co-workers, baptize those who profess a faith in Jesus, and more. You are likely to have more access into your field of work than the pastor of a church.

A Holistic View of Mission: Changing The World

Another major implication of holistic thinking is how we view involvement with non-believers. This significantly effects how we live out the Great Commission. In John 17 Jesus asked His Father for all those who followed Him to be in the world but not of it. It is one of the few times Jesus clarifies himself to God the Father. He emphasizes, *"Father, I don't mean that you should take them out of the world."* (John 17:15) His emphasis was for us rather than God the Father.

It is often taught God wants you to separate from the world to be Holy. This is a dualistic way of thinking about holiness. God's concept of holiness is to be set apart from the world while still being immersed in it. This is impossible apart from daily dependence on the Holy Spirit.

Jesus exemplified holistic vision in His ministry. He constantly spent time with people who the religious leaders of his day deemed more sinful than average. Jesus spent time with tax collectors, prostitutes, adulterers, and even Gentiles. As a result, He was constantly accused of being impure. It was a dualistic guilt-by-association thought pattern which still exists today. What did Jesus say in response? *"I have come for the sick not the healthy. I came to call sinners."* (Mark 2:17)

We should take our example from Jesus rather than the Pharisees. If no area is off limits to His redemption, we can stop creating separatist Christian ghettos. If we continue to do this, our social structures and businesses will get darker because the true bringers of light only seek to gather together. Christians should once again be the best architects, artists, lawyers, street cleaners, and public servants.

Conclusion

Believers graduating from college with this holistic worldview is crucial to successful transition to life after college. When students gain this mindset, they will move from seeking to find God in their workplace to bringing God into their careers. They will move from just leading spiritual activities at church to taking church into the marketplace. We will graduate workers who aren't looking for good places to drink, but who are empowered to create the very wells that give others the living water.

As graduates see God meet them in the darkest places, and see Him redeem what they previously felt were 'secular' arenas, then Jesus will ultimately show there is no transition at all. Holistic Christians take the Kingdom of God with them wherever they go so they can't drop out of the Kingdom. In this way, God will show that He is equally active and present in college as He is in life after school. There is no division after all.

Questions for Discussion:

1. What are some occupations in which you think a Christian should not work?

2. What areas of society around you does God want to redeem?

3. What are some "walls" that your ministry or church has built that separate the "professional" and the "ordinary" believer?

4. What are some things that you can do that will help model Christ in the areas of society where there is little of His Light?

Jeremy Story
President, Campus Renewal Ministries
www.campusrenewal.org

Jeremy lives in New York City with his wife and six children. He is the national President of Campus Renewal Ministries and serves on the boards of several other ministries. He and Campus Renewal Ministries have a passion for building simple churches and united prayer movements on college campuses. To this end, he has worked on hundreds of campuses in over 40 states and 5 continents.

CHAPTER 12
Experiencing God At Work

by Craig Seibert

In this chapter, we want to explore how you can intimately experience God in your work life. To start with, we will set up a framework for how you can look for God's activities in your work life and then, as the chapter concludes, we will give several examples.

As we all know, in today's world, invisible radio, TV, and digital waves are all around us, and if we have the right equipment and knowledge of how it operates, we can tune into this invisible world to hear and see some incredible things.

The Bible makes it clear that the God of the universe is similarly at work all around us every day. If we take the time to tune in and observe what is going on around us, we can see Him at work in some incredible ways. Even more rewarding is the fact that He is not just some impersonal force, but a personal God that knows us, our personality, our concerns, our problems, our needs, our joys, and even what we are going to face each and every day.

Our challenge in the busyness of life is to get tuned in and to watch our daily lives through both physical eyes and spiritual eyes, so that we might have the opportunity to see and experience God on a daily basis.

Regular Fresh Encounter

The starting point for experiencing God in this way is for you to have some kind of regular encounter with the God that made you. The Bible is called the Living Word for a reason, in that the living God of the universe can actually speak to our hearts through its pages.

When the habit of scripture intake and prayer is cultivated on a regular basis, God can fill you up with what you need for the day. God also uses this time to prepare your heart to experience Him during the day and to be able to see Him at work. When filled up in this way, we also seem to become more aware of how God creates opportunities for us to encourage and help others.

Ways That God Shows Up In Your Actual Work

With this established starting point, we can then enter our workplace with greater "God awareness". We can tune into God's activity. We can watch how He seems to order and guide our days in the world of work as we yield ourselves to Him. Here are some of the ways Christ followers have observed God at work in their lives while on the job. They have seen God:

- Allow them to reach and connect with people they need to do their job well

- Allow others to reach and connect with them (often with perfect timing)

- Navigate them around some problems and some situations that would hinder their effectiveness for the day

- Give them favor in their supervisors' and peers' eyes

- Still allow some problems to help develop and mature them, as well as, put His power and glory on display to those around them as they handle problems well

- Give them creativity, clarity, wisdom, and focus

- Give them His love for others in their world of work

- Give them spiritual insight into people's lives and situations they face

God does not have to do these things. Yet, His activity is going on all around us, and He loves to reveal Himself to those who genuinely love Him and seek Him.

Ways that God Wants to Use You in the Lives of Others

Another way that God wants you to experience Him at your work is how He wants to use you in the lives of others. You see, God *assigns people* to your workplace because He knows you are there and can minister to their needs. Here are some of the ways you can know God is working in the lives of others and how He may be providing an opening for you to be involved in their lives:*

- *Felt Need or Spiritual Things - Anytime someone shares a personal problem, crisis or need, in earnest, you can be confident that God is at work in that situation trying to draw the person closer to Himself.*

- *Leading of God's Spirit - You can stay attentive to the Holy Spirit, and He will allow you to hear the needs in your place of work (the Holy Spirit's role is to speak; our role is to listen).*

- *Prayer, Care and Share - Those not currently expressing a need may not be as open to talking about God on the surface, but through prayer, care, and taking the initiative to ask questions and share Christ's love, it may result in someone sharing a felt need or bringing up a spiritual need or question.*

By faith, step into these invitations by God to be a part of what He is doing.

Staying God Aware

As you find yourself becoming more "God Aware" in your work, you will experience a new level of faith and work integration. You will begin to see how prayer actually fits into the rhythm of your work life. Remember prayer is both talking and listening to God. Here are just a few ideas that you might try:

- *Pray as you start the day at your desk.*

- *Pray as you make phone calls to customers or answer emails.*

- *Pray as you walk down the hallway or by people's cubes or offices.*

- *Pray as you sit in meetings for the people and for the situation being discussed.*

- *Pray as you participate in management meetings or as one is going on in your area.*

- *Pray that God might fulfill His highest purpose for your business or company.*

Keep a Workplace Journal

One of the perceived problems with Christianity today is that there is nothing about it from the non-believer's perspective that reveals God's supernatural activity. Meanwhile, people of faith have God encounters frequently, but they so quickly forget them, or write them off, as just circumstance or luck.

A **Workplace Journal** helps you build your faith in God as you make notes to yourself and clearly identify the ways you see God at work in your life, particularly in the workplace. This, in turn, not only encourages you, but serves as a witness to others around you, as you can confidently share how God is at work regularly in your life. Entries in a **Workplace Journal** might include:

- **Peace** - In the midst of tough circumstances

- **Clarity and Creativity** - For new product, service or solution

- **Sovereign Connection** - Where you meet someone unexpectedly or connect with someone easily that you need to reach, and they help you with a specific situation you were facing. A sovereign connection can also occur when those that need to reach you are getting through for your benefit and theirs.

- **Problem Avoidance** - After the fact, you find God moved you around a problem or prevented a problem.

- **Spiritual Conversation** - Someone expressed a need that has a spiritual root, or you felt inclined to say something that opened the door to discuss spiritual things.

- **Holy Spirit** - You just know God guided you in a particular direction or situation.

Keep your Workplace Journal on your desk (or work area) and make a note whenever you see any "God Activity" around you while on the job. The more you do this, the more you will see Him at work. Leave your Journal at your desk overnight so that it is always there, and you do not forget it or fall out of the habit of using it. Review it from time to time, and you will be greatly encouraged.

Workplace Journal Entries

Below are some entries in my workplace journal. The exciting thing for me is that this entire list all occurred in a one-month period. When you look for God, you really can see Him at work. I am reminded that these are not random occurrences that happen every year or two. They are happening all the time!

Peace – I was out of town on a business trip, and I woke up at 5:17a.m. I was strongly impressed that when I got up, I was to look up 1 Thessalonians 5:17. When I did, I read this: *"Be joyful always; ^{17} pray continually; ^{18} give thanks in all circumstances, for this is God's will for you in Christ Jesus." 1 Thessalonians 5:16-18*

This greatly encouraged me as I was going through some hard changes at work. But God further wanted to endorse His word to me. Upon arriving at home, I shared this little happening with my wife and two children, 10 and 8. My sons face lit up. "Dad, that is the verse we are memorizing at school!" Amazingly, out of all the verses in the Bible, God had my son memorizing this exact verse. By way of further endorsement from God, the next morning I opened a PowerPoint™. presentation that I had created two years ago about the history of the Pilgrims at Thanksgiving. The central verse of the whole presentation? You guessed it – 1 Thessalonians 5:17. God gave me this verse and endorsed it through two additional providential circumstances. Thank you, Lord.

Clarity and Creativity – On a recent trip, a friend, Eric, and I were going to do a presentation to a group of leaders on a new concept of gathering people together that we were calling an "organic network." Our plan was to spend 25 minutes verbally sharing what we had learned and then interacting with the group on the topic. The night before our presentation, we had two different conversations that highlighted the fact that these concepts needed to be presented visually so that they could be better understood. God began to provide a flood of ideas on how this might be shared visually. From 9p.m. to 11p.m., God provided clarity and insight in how to organize the material visually in a PowerPoint™. God provided in two hours, what would normally have taken two or three days to think through. Thank you, Lord.

Sovereign Connections – On another recent trip, I was in a conference, and my friend, Dave, walked in right before we were about to start and offered me half of an egg, bacon, and cheese bagel. I said "sure." Man, it was good. I said, "Where did you get that?, I have to go there tomorrow morning!" The next morning, I headed over to the bagel shop and ordered my bagel and coffee and sat down to think and journal about some challenges I was facing in my work life. No sooner had I sat down, and a dear friend, whom I had not even realized was at the conference, walked by the window of the shop and walked in. I said, "Tracy, what are you doing here?". He said, "I was just out walking around, seeing if I could find a place to eat and walked by this place, so decided to come in. May I join you?". "Yeah, man!", I said. For the next 45 minutes, we were able to discuss the issues I was facing, his perspective on things, and how to make sense of them in light of God's big picture. An amazing providential happening orchestrated by my loving heavenly father. Thank you, Lord.

Problem Avoidance – For a number of years, I have served on a leadership team of a national organization. The organization is going through some leadership and directional changes currently which has for the moment displaced me from the leadership team, yet many of my responsibilities remain unchanged. This has actually been to my benefit. My time has been freed up to really focus on some strategic planning and relationship building in my specific responsibility area. If I had been left on the organizational chart for this national team during its transition period, much of my time would have been spent in other discussions and decision making that others are quite capable at doing. Thank you, Lord, for protecting my time and for the specific ministry assignments you have given to me.

Spiritual Conversation – On a hotel shuttle bus, I found myself as the only passenger with Michael, the driver. I try to be friendly in those situations and talk to the driver a bit. In asking how his day was going, he revealed that he was having problems with his shoulder that have existed for some time. I tried to empathize with this pain, but did not really know what further questions to ask, so we naturally transitioned to other things. Upon arriving at the hotel, Michael parked the van a few yards back from the entrance, and I had a strong impression to ask him if I could pray for his shoulder. His face lit up as he said, "Absolutely!" So I prayed and shared with him some encouraging words to pursue God, make Him first in his life, and consider the claims of Christ. I gave him my business card and reference to a website where people could investigate spiritual things in a non-threatening environment. I have prayed for Michael several times as he has come to mind since that trip. Thank you, Lord, for this opportunity.

Holy Spirit – Since becoming a Christian, I have become very interested in how God intersects with humankind during the course of history. My particular interest has even become more focused on God's Providences in the Plymouth Pilgrims and in the Revolutionary War period. This, in turn, has created a deep interest in the Declaration of Independence and the U.S. Constitution. Over the years, I have created some unique training videos on these topics.

Over a several week period, the Holy Spirit began to steadily and gently press into my heart and mind that some of this content should be produced in YOUTUBE friendly format and put out there for free. As, I prayerfully considered this, God really confirmed it in my heart as a direction He was leading me to take.

So I published the content to YOUTUBE. The results have been amazing – at least to me. In a four-month period, over 2,500 people have trained themselves in Understanding the Declaration of Independence and the U.S. Constitution**. God has connected me with many new Christian leaders. God has used the content in others' lives to write training curriculum for churches, and some foundations have become interested in our work. This has been a "pay-it-forward" experience for me. Give it away for free at God's prompting, but then see what He does with it. Thank you Lord.

Conclusion
God is at work all around us and in our world of work. Let's join Him in that work and record it in our workplace journals as encouragement to ourselves and to others.

Questions for Discussion:

1. Share an example of a "felt need" of one of your co-workers or fellow students from this week.

2. Is there a person at work or school to whom you have become more sensitive this week?

3. Has a co-worker or classmate requested prayer for anyone recently?

4. How do you remind yourself to be God's representative each day?

Craig Seibert
www.cmseibert@mindspring.com

Craig Seibert has been on staff with Campus Crusade's marketplace ministry for over 10 years and currently serves with the Graduating Seniors Team and Internet Equipping Team. Craig is passionate about seeing college seniors transition well into their full-time vocational worklife and helping them experience God in the midst of their work. Craig lives in Charlotte, NC with his wife, Rebecca and two children.

* I would like to acknowledge Dr. Henry Blackaby's, "Experiencing God Workbook" that was first published in the middle 1980s, as a ground breaking work on some of these concepts.

**To see these videos, type "Keys to Understanding the Declaration" or "Keys to Understanding the Constitution" in the search box at www.youtube.com.

CHAPTER 13
Transportable Faith

by Dave Riner

"Dave, you'd make a great missionary."

This might have been true, but I was headed to the corporate world.

When my friend, Trey, said this to me – the spring before I finished my MBA – I was both flattered and confused. I had a mixed record of faithfulness in college, yet I hoped God would use my life. Could he use me in the business world?

The question dogged me as I moved my new bride and our old stuff from my college town to my new career town three hours away. I was entering the work force with a large petroleum company. My wife, Rhea Lana, and I didn't know anyone in town or at work. We were starting from scratch.

I woke up before my first work day feeling nervous. During my time with God that morning, I felt Him challenge me. "Dave, if they ask you to compromise today, will you keep My standards, even if it costs you your job?" I struggled with the answer. It was a year in which the job market was tight. I had searched for six months to finally get hired. I remembered two years earlier, during a summer job, my bosses had placed me in an unethical spot. It was painful then to do the right thing. Starting from scratch again? The thought made my stomach turn. I went to work half expecting my career would end before lunchtime.

Instead, friendly people were willing to help a new guy find the notebook paper and the water fountain. I ended the day with pens, a phone, and the promise of a computer within the week. My work associates began training me to interpret contracts, settle payments, and do business in the oil industry. So began four years as a young engineer in Oklahoma, followed by four more years as a slightly older engineer in the Texas Panhandle.

During those eight years I was faced with a very basic question. "How do I live as a believer at work? I wanted not only to survive as a believer, but actually grow in Christ. And, if possible, I wanted to impact others. I had helped students grow spiritually while ministering on the campus. Could such a thing happen in the suburbs and around the water cooler at work?

Honestly, I had no idea. My college ministry had faded in the distance as I drove westward to my corporate job. Gone were the familiar friends to encourage me and hold me accountable. Also gone was the upbeat collegiate worship style; I discovered that churches were more traditional in my new town. My spiritual leaders disappeared in the rear view mirror as well.

TRANSPORT YOUR FAITH

In order to have a chance at surviving spiritually in the working world, I needed to *rebuild the positive forces in my life.* That's the first thing I would tell you if you find yourself in a similar spot. First, have a *transportable* faith. College is an incredible time to grow like never before. Congratulations, if you have used your campus as a "spiritual incubator" – a place to develop knowledge, character, skills, and vision in a community of like-minded friends. You've got a good foundation on which to build your life.

But, you can't be passive. Letting life happen to you in the "real world" will leave you a sitting duck for compromise and spiritual failure. If you are in a new place, you are very vulnerable. There can be a lot of corporate peer pressure when a young employee enters a new workplace. Everyone is watching to see what you are made of. Of course they want to know if you can do the job, but they are also curious about your character. And you'll have plenty of opportunities to show it, so get ready! Profanity, dirty jokes, temptations like cutting out early or showing up late, pilfering office supplies, stretching an expense reimbursement, shady clubs on business trips, talking bad about the boss or fellow employees – the list of potential pitfalls goes on and on!

I learned over time that *every day* on the job was just like my first day – a test to see if I would honor God with my life while at work. I needed to be close to Him to handle it. A transportable faith is possible because, thankfully, God is always there waiting anytime we make a transition. This was true for Abraham when he relocated. It is true today. The Father loves his children and wants our best. He wants a wonderful and fruitful life for you – even more than you do!

When I think back on that question, "Dave, will you come home if ...?" I believe God was basically asking, "Do you trust me? Are we doing this together?" From that question can come a life partnership. As the Lord walked with Adam in the cool of the day, He wants to walk with us. He was waiting for me in my new cubical on the ninth floor. He went with me to every meeting. He was there when we moved to Borger, Texas, and when my wife had our baby boy at the truck stop in Amarillo. In the office, out at the refinery, with the wild turkeys and pheasants on the oil lease – God was there. *"I will never leave you; never will I forsake you."* Hebrews 13:5. That is His promise.

To transport your faith, you also need to find fellowship at work. Back at my first job, I heard about a corporate lawyer in the building next door. His name was Steve. On Tuesdays, he invited believers to eat a sandwich in his office at lunch. The guys who showed up shared from their hearts and prayed together among the mountains of law books. I looked forward to those times since they were an oasis in a corporate spiritual desert. Steve's office was a place to rest, get perspective, and gain strength.

You also need to find fellowship in the community. College ministries are effective in reaching students who can't seem to get themselves to a church.

Yet, God's ultimate design for you is fellowshipping with your local church. If you aren't in one, or looking for one, well, you are unplugged from what He is doing! Unless you are a pioneer missionary, there is a body of believers near you.

Such a fellowship may not be like your college group or your contemporary church in your college town. Transporting your faith means rebuilding the warm, familiar place you just left. You'll have to meet new people in other stages of life. It does not happen overnight, and part of your maturity is accepting the imperfections you can clearly see in today's church. These warts are similar to the warts in the first wave of churches in the Bible. Half the New Testament was written to imperfect churches and people!

The secret is your taking the initiative to put God, people, spiritual habits, and ministry back into your life. You have to set up shop, spiritually. You will be surprised as the Lord places new people in your life – people from many different walks and life experiences. Since no one really knows you, it is tempting to fall into the shadows when you go to a new place. Instead, lean forward. Transport your faith.

BE AN INFLUENCER

Second, make a decision. Will I lead, or will I follow?

The people in my new church were a blessing. They were real people trying to lean on God and make it through life. Everywhere I have lived – Arkansas, Oklahoma, Texas, Tennessee, and California – the same is true. God's people are like sheep struggling to listen and follow the Shepherd. They are very precious to Him.

When I looked around at church people, I discovered something. I, the new guy, was having a fairly regular time with God. However, Bob, the physical therapist, was not. While I was familiar with accountability partners asking me tough questions (i.e. pornography and integrity questions), James the banker was not. I knew how to share the gospel, but Joe the accountant did not (and didn't really want to learn!). I also knew that God placed a priority on reaching every nation with the gospel. Did anyone at church know a missionary by name? A few did.

It's not that I was mature in my faith. Far from it! I was just a twenty-something, struggling to seek the Lord. It seemed as though a version of *Gulliver's Travels* was happening. Back on the campus, I felt like a spiritual Lilliputian – very small compared to my more faithful college friends. But now in my new home town, I suddenly seemed like a spiritual giant! I discovered that at my church – in the area of spiritual disciplines – I was hitting the 90th percentile without really trying. Even among the deacons and elders, very few seemed to be actively pursuing an evangelistic ministry. Not many in the church seemed willing to commit to the spiritual pursuits I had grown accustomed to on campus. A huge difference in standards existed.

It was a dangerous place to be. First, spiritual pride and a judgmental attitude against the apathy I observed were temptations. While it is important to challenge believers to a high standard, coming on too strong can do more damage than good! I risked alienating good people by overheating them with my standards.

Another danger was a lack of spiritual leadership in my life. It would have been incredible if a mentor had been available to help me navigate through relationships at work, at church, and in my neighborhood. Left to myself, I made some sophomore mistakes. I was suddenly among people in all walks of life – middle-aged men, lady divorcees, high-powered executives, low-powered lazies, grandmothers, older singles, pretend atheists, and nerds of all ages. How was I to make an impact on such a diverse group? My ministry toolbox had only a few things in it that worked great in the dormitory. Using the same "opening lines," or pamphlets in the corporate atmosphere seemed clunky. Trial and error humbled me. I was inexperienced in measuring my relationships and weaving spiritual truth into them.

Besides pride and mistakes, a third danger was looming large – the danger of complacency. The Enemy can use our past ministry mistakes and the apathy of others to discourage us. Feelings of unworthiness can cut into our will to step out and persevere in laboring. If we aren't careful, we will eventually quit trying to make an impact for Christ in our world altogether. We will cease being leaders and ooze into the low standards and expectations which are prevalent around us. These preventers can sideline someone who used to be somewhat effective back on the campus. To me, complacency is the worst danger of them all. Once we settle on a low spiritual standard, we are very likely to never raise it – *for the rest of our lives!*

As I close out my chapter, here are a few things for the "ministry tool box" I mentioned earlier. These are a few things that I wish someone had told me when it comes to skillfully influencing others for Christ at work.

- Fly your flag *early* instead of *often* when you meet new people. I've found that it is easier to let folks know that I am a believer sometime early in our relationship. That way they know what to say and not say in front of me. Really, I am trying to save *them* some embarrassment! You shouldn't start every sentence with, "Praise the Lord!" But, when you get a chance to talk about your life, bring your faith into the discussion as soon as you can. Then, act natural, be friendly, and talk about the NFL.

- Pray for your work associates. And let them help you. It is not hard to spend time with someone during break or at lunch and say, "Leonard, I am trying to work on praying more and better. You could really help me. Would you have one or two things I could pray for you about? You'd be doing me a favor. Thanks!" Few (if any) of your workmates would respond negatively to that. On the contrary, they are much more likely to be appreciative and warm. That can get the ball rolling toward a spiritual conversation sometime in the future.

- Be curious about all parts of the lives of your co-workers – including their spiritual life. Ask about the things that are important to them. The more curious you are, the more naturally you can broach spiritual topics. *Everyone* has spiritual interest. The question is whether they trust talking about it with you. Really, they will take their cue from you. If you are curious instead of nervous, they will probably be very open.

- Learn a great way to share the gospel. You want something that is a *dialogue,* not a one-way, preachy monologue. You want a lot of, "Could I get your opinion about this?" You want to ask them along the way, "So, does that make sense?"

Well, twenty years later I'm still not a missionary (though missionaries are my heroes!). One thing is for sure, my eight corporate years were a journey in faith I will never forget. I made lifetime friends and learned lifetime lessons. Those early decisions flavored the rest of my life and formed the foundation of who I am today.

Who are you, and who do you want to be? Take these chapters to heart. Make good decisions now. They will impact you and your family for the rest of your life.

Questions for Discussion:

1. Are you in a regular small group? What are the benefits of being in it?
2. Do you currently have a mentor or two in your life? What are the benefits?
3. What are the things that cause you to be spiritually proud?
4. Are there any signs of complacency at this time in your spiritual journey?

Dave Riner
www.driner@stumo.org

Dave Riner, 47, has been Executive Director of Student Mobilization since January 2000. Dave is also Chairman of the Board of The Traveling Team. Dave is a graduate of Vanderbilt University and completed a Masters in Business Administration at the University of Arkansas. Before coming to StuMo fourteen years ago, Dave worked eight years as an engineer for Phillips Petroleum Company. Dave is married to Rhea Lana, and they have three children: Bekah, Ben, and Leah.

CHAPTER 14

Transitioning Young Adults from Collegiate Ministry to the Real World

by Dave Edwards

My name is Dave Edwards. I worked with a major collegiate ministry on a university campus for fifteen years. I now pastor a church in that same city, and the church is well populated by the students from that university. Being a pastor is my vocation and calling. Equipping collegians with the Word of God and helping them to get ready to do the work of the ministry in the real world is my passion.

As I endeavor to have excellence in my work, I have found my best tutors to be the Holy Spirit and the young adults He has given me to mentor. I have learned to ask questions and to listen carefully as they give brutally honest answers. I have asked such pointed questions as:

1. How ready do you feel to face the responsibilities of life after college?

2. How confident are you at applying what you have learned in your collegiate ministry training, to your new challenges in life?

3. How able do you perceive your church to be at equipping you to succeed in life?

4. When you don't find your church sufficiently meeting your needs, where do you go for help?

I also learned that I am not the only one asking important questions. Several years ago I drafted a set of questions that I heard them asking. I have revised it numerous times as I've listened again and again to their fears and their dreams. These questions, and the answers, will shape much of what their future will become.

I pray that you, Reader, will consider these ideas that your peers have expressed. Prayerfully seek God's answers for your own life and circumstances. He will faithfully reveal truth to you, as He has done for generations who have sought Him. He has a plan for your life that includes Himself, and He will not only reveal it to you, but will provide the means to accomplish it.

13 Questions Young Adults Need to Answer Before They Turn 30

1. "Do I have a firm grasp on the basic doctrines of the Christian faith?"

   Young adults will live and minister in an age that prides itself on uncertainty. It is imperative that you learn Biblical truth in a clear and accurate manner, and that you know how to study and interpret the Scripture. Begin by learning the skill of inductive Bible study. Next, over time, accumulate reliable study tools such as a study Bible, a Bible dictionary/encyclopedia, and a growing array of Bible commentaries. Along the way – with the guidance of a more experienced Bible study such as your pastor – begin accumulating time-tested works on theology that will give you quick and useful answers to questions you encounter.

2. "Do I know how to walk in the fullness of the Holy Spirit?"

   The future and fruitfulness of an individual is not a matter of personality, training, or intellect as much as it is one of knowing how to walk in the fullness of Christ. Jesus was emphatic when He said, "apart from Me you can do nothing." 'Nothing' is the outcome of a life lived apart from Christ, a life lived in the energy of the flesh. On the other hand, a person who lives consistently and wholeheartedly in Christ will experience what Jesus describes as "fruitful". (John 15:5) In fact, his life will be disproportionately influential, which is what

Jesus calls bearing "much fruit".

Walking in the fullness of the Holy Spirit is description of a life that consistently seeks Christ, listens to Christ, and obeys Christ. The ability to do this flows out of the heart that thirsts for Him, seeks Him, and trusts Him.

Practicing spiritual disciplines does not result in walking in the fullness of the Holy Spirit. However, individuals who know Christ well and live in His fullness are those who have developed habits of Scripture intake, prayer, fellowship, and service. These mature followers do not confuse spiritual discipline with abiding. Yet, they grasp the close connection that diligence in spiritual intake has with fostering a responsive heart. And so, it is basic to this matter of walking in the Holy Spirit to be an individual who routinely learns and applies the Scripture, who regularly prays in sincere and trusting manner, and who consistently gathers with growing believers for the purpose of worship, study, and encouragement.

3. "Do I know how to restore my soul when I am spiritually depleted?"

One remarkable quality in the life of David was his ability to reassemble his spiritual life when it got knocked off the shelf. (see 1 Samuel 30:6) Many of the Psalms credited to him are his written effort to realign his inner being with the will and heart of God in the midst of deep spiritual confusion, desperation, danger, and loneliness. The brilliant thing about this young man was that he knew how to develop the strength of his soul during normal times, *and* he knew how to recover the strength of his soul during difficult times.

If you intend to be a young man or woman who is going to have endurance for a lifetime of walking with God, you need to know both how to feed your soul and how to restore your soul.

4. "Do I know what it is to be a maturing man/woman?"

Masculinity and femininity are concepts that need to be reclaimed and clarified if young adults are to transition into individuals with a strong grasp on what it means to be a man or a woman. Masculinity in particular has come on hard times with the breakdown of the American family, the absent father, and the feminizing of our culture.

Paul put it this way, *"When I was a child, I talked like a child, I thought like a child, I reasoned like a child. When I became a man, I put childish ways behind me."* (1 Corinthians 13:11 NIV) Have you identified the difference between childishness and maturity? Have you resolved to put childish ways behind you and accept the responsible patterns of mature manhood and mature womanhood?

5. "Do I have a clear life mission, and do I know how to use it to navigate life choices?"

This question is critical if you desire to transition into the real world with strength and stamina.

Too often 'life mission' is expressed in terms of ministry slogans ('to know Christ and make Him known' or 'to reach my world for Christ'). These obviously have a place in Christian conversation. But you need to expand your understanding of what you uniquely bring to life and how it fits into your mission. You need to be able to express your unique visions, designs, and roles. Then, tackle the hard work of learning how to chart a reasonable course for life, how to evaluate progress and failure, and, how to make mid-course corrections. This valuable exercise is often easier if done with the guidance of a mentor, pastor, or other trusted ministry leader.

6. "Am I ready to enter and develop a flourishing marriage relationship?"

   The world will only erode your ideas about marriage unless you have clear Biblical footing in this area. You need to seek out what the Bible says about marital success, and identify someone to whom you can go for wisdom when needed. Even if you aren't married, start gathering insight into the components of an enduring, growing relationship. *"By wisdom a house is built and through understanding it is established; through knowledge its rooms are filled with rare and beautiful treasures."* (Proverbs 24:3-4)

7. "What does it mean to be financially free?"

   Do you have a Biblical perspective on financial management? Have you developed a reasonable strategy for financial freedom? Look for courses and books, such as those offered by Dave Ramsey. Take advantage of church offered classes such as "Financial Peace University", by Dave Ramsey, or "Crown Ministries", a ten-week course in financial freedom.

8. "Do I know how to hold down a job and help an employer be successful?"

   Young adults need a sound, Biblical work ethic. Spend some time with a Christian person who models this work ethic, and ask them questions. Find out what the real challenges are in the workplace. Seek to be a worker whose testimony on the job is enhanced by your competence in your field.

9. "Do I know how to honor my parents now that I am on my own?"

   Ephesians 6:2 tells us to "honor your father and mother (which is the first commandment with a promise)." With the growing collapse of the American home has come an ambiguity about how to honor parents, especially once you leave home. Covenant in your heart to excel in this virtue.

10. "Do I know how to manage time in order to accomplish goals?"

If you have not yet mastered this skill by the time you graduate, or if you tend to procrastinate, it is definitely time to spend time with someone who can show you how to use a priority time management system. Ask that person not only to show you how to do it, but to meet with you once a month for three months to help you establish a habit. This will help you for the rest of your life.

11. "Am I honest about my secret sins/weaknesses?"

Every young adult struggles with something. Some are actually failing, but cannot bring themselves to admit it to someone. Others may not be failing, but there may be some question about their personal adequacy that leaves them seemingly powerless at times.

One of the most helpful ways to strengthen yourself against such an inner battle is to build safe, open and constructive relationships with a few peers. This may take the form of a small group that applies the Scripture together, prays for one another, accepts/corrects one another, and bears with one another. Some of these relationships may need to remain intact for 2-3 years before a high level of trust is developed. Once trust is established, there is a new weapon at your disposal that enables you to walk out of defeat and weakness toward victory and strength.

12. "Do I know how to develop relationships in my world which attract people to follow Christ?"

This is evangelism. People do it differently. Most of the young adults I talk with come out of their college ministry with tremendous training in personal evangelism. Then, after a few months on the job and in a neighborhood, and after a few initial attempts to identify with Christ, they find themselves asking, 'now what?'

We are observing two broad trends in our evangelism training. First, young adults want to be endorsed in the style of evangelism that fits them best. Some are confronters (they witness to everything), some are intercessors, some invite people to events where the gospel is shared, some are servants, and some are at their best when part of a larger event or strategy. Undoubtedly, there are additional styles beyond these. They need to know that what comes naturally to them in reaching out to their world is valid. If they are continually expected to express evangelism in one way, many will put evangelism on hold because it seems awkward to them.

A second trend we see is in the area of servant evangelism. More and more young adults are excited about the idea of community service and charitable deeds as a form of outreach to their community. If this is true in your situation, release yourself to put this motivation into action. Not only does this minister to the needy in your community, it may become a convenient way to engage your skeptical peers, who also feel a sense of duty to their community and will join their Christian friends in these serving events. It becomes a great way to build bridges to both the community and your unbelieving friends.

13. "Do I know how to benefit others in the body of Christ by serving and using my spiritual gift(s)?"

Many (perhaps most) young adults have very little idea of where they fit in the larger body of Christ. If you are one of these, getting help to answer this question in your 20's will do much to build your vision, confidence, and motivation for ministry the rest of your life.

Your first decade out of college is one of the most vital in your life. Come at it proactively rather than simply taking what comes your way. You obviously do not have control over your future. However, you can be ready for your future. You can use your 20's to chart a plan that will have you ready at 30 for the adventure that awaits you. My advice to you would be what I give the young men and women in our church…ask the right questions, and be relentless at getting wise answers. Start with the 13 questions I have discussed here. Add to the list as you see fit. Then, with the help of the Lord along with wise mentors, begin your quest of gathering wisdom and applying it as fully as possible.

Proverbs 1:7 NIV
The fear of the LORD is the beginning of knowledge,
but fools despise wisdom and discipline.

Proverbs 3:7-8 NIV
Do not be wise in your own eyes;
fear the LORD and shun evil.
This will bring health to your body
and nourishment to your bones.

Proverbs 2:1-6 NIV
My son, if you accept my words and store up my commands within you,
turning your ear to wisdom and applying your heart to understanding,
and if you call out for insight and cry aloud for understanding,
and if you look for it as for silver and search for it as for hidden treasure,
then you will understand the fear of the LORD and find the knowledge of God.
For the LORD gives wisdom, and from his mouth come knowledge and understanding.

Questions for Discussion:

1. Which of the 13 questions is the most difficult for you to answer, and why?

2. How would you answer question number 3 regarding "restoring your soul"?

3. What are you currently doing to honor your parents?

4. Do you have someone with whom you can share your personal challenges?

Dave Edwards
dedwards@riverchurchnorman.org

David Edwards is a church planter with River Church in Norman, Oklahoma. He has been ministering with young adults for thirty years, and has served on staff of both collegiate ministries and local churches. He is currently focused on mobilizing young adults for church planting both in the U.S. and internationally. He and his wife, Nancy, have four children and two grandchildren.

CHAPTER 15

Building Your Life, as You are Establishing Your Career

by Chuck Price

As you begin your career in the marketplace, you are probably doing so with high hopes and expectations of living out your faith and values and making a meaningful impact with your life.

But life can get in your way. And you can inadvertently get stuck trying to make it all work. Whether it is the opportunities that come along or the lack of them, the demands and challenges of getting established, or all of the unexpected things that happen along the way, activities have a way of becoming their own task masters.

And before you know it, you find yourself operating more as a "Human Doer" rather than a "Human Being." Or you become like the person who, grappling with the emptiness of his life, says, "I was climbing the ladder of success only to find that it was leaning against the wrong wall!"

Being a person who reflects God's image and lives out His redemptive plan for those around you takes intentionality.

I have found in my own life, as well as in interacting with the many men and women I have been able to encourage along the way, that there are some basic guiding principles to keep in mind on the journey. And there are also some frequent pitfalls that we can so easily fall into that we should take note to keep away from them.

Three common traps to avoid:

1. Allowing My Work to Become my Identity

Work can and should be fulfilling. That's the way God designed it. However, it should never be the sole definer of who I am. When that begins to happen, I am unwittingly being drawn into a subtle form of idolatry.

All of us have run into people whose whole lives revolve around their jobs. All of their conversation, their think time, and most of their relationships are work related. For these people, there are usually huge areas of their lives that just don't work so well. Whether it is their spouses or their children, the effect of their one-dimensional life takes its toll. But what happens when their job is no longer there?

God ordained work, and doing it well is a form of worship. In fact, the standard is excellence, Col 3:23-24 says: *"Whatever you do, do your work heartily, as for the Lord rather than for men; knowing that from the Lord you will receive the reward of the inheritance. It is the Lord Christ whom you serve."* (NASB)

Remember though that God meant for life to be relational. From the very beginning, the story of God's creation of man, the fall, and redemption is all about relationship. And we are the most fulfilled when we are in right relationship with God and right relationship with one another in the context of a community of faith.

Suggestions to Avoid this Trap

- Actively build a few relationships into your schedule that are outside of a work context (i.e. small group Bible study, church, service group, athletic league).

- Seek to listen to cues from those closest to you that you are being unhealthy.

- Know when to turn it off – whether it is a Blackberry, a cell phone, or the pre-occupied sense of intensity that lets everyone around you know that you're "not present at the moment". Recognize when "enough is enough", and take the time to wind down.

2. Allowing the Crises of the Moment to Control My Life.

It sounds something like this: "This is just a temporary season where I can't afford to have a life because of the demands of the job!" Or: "If I can just make it through the next several months of intensity, then things will settle down, and I will get connected with my family, my friends, and get in a place where I can focus more on my walk with the Lord."

This is a huge trap because it is so often very cleverly disguised! It is surrounded by the many urgent demands where the vital things of life keep getting put off and delayed by a seemingly endless stream of crises and the immediacy of the moment.

When a person's life is continually dominated by urgency, they run the risk of becoming an adrenaline junky and developing a false sense of their own importance. And when a real crisis comes along, they have no credibility, particularly with their family and close friends (if there are any!). They used the crises excuse one too many times and ended up neglecting their most important relationships.

Suggestions to Avoid this Trap

Learn to recognize pressures of the workplace for what they are: pressures in the workplace! That's normal – but to treat every new pressure or challenge as a crisis is abnormal and ultimately unproductive.

Learn to objectify the challenges/opportunities you are presented with by developing a short list of questions to evaluate their relative urgency. (i.e.

"Where is the sense of pressure I am feeling coming from?" "Is this project or assignment really that urgent?" "If it is, what can I do to rearrange the other things I am doing and focus in a more undivided way on this project?")

Take time to identify the habits or patterns that help you be more productive and seek to actively build them into your routine. Likewise, seek to develop an awareness of what makes you unproductive so that you can self-correct when you find yourself just "spinning your wheels" in activity, working harder and harder without increasing your effectiveness.

3. Waiting to Live out My Faith in the Workplace.

"I will wait till I am established in the job before I let anyone know that I am a Christian." This is a common misconception that many fall into. It is the incorrect thinking that "until the time is right, it is best to hang back and fit in".

The real truth is that the longer you wait to let people know that you are a follower of Christ either by your words or actions, the harder it is to do so.

When I was working with naval officers some years ago, they would often tell me that when they were assigned to a new ship, if they did not let their fellow officers in the ward room know in some way that they were a follower of Christ when they first arrived, that it then became increasingly difficult because they had already compromised their values in some way.

Remember Jesus said, *"You are the world's light—a city on a hill, glowing in the night for all to see. Don't hide your light! Let it shine for all; let your good deeds glow for all to see, so that they will praise your heavenly Father."* (Matthew 5:15-16, The Living Bible)

Suggestions to Avoid this Trap

- Remind yourself daily that God has placed you in your unique sphere of influence to serve Him and reflect his love and care to those with whom you come into contact.

- Be others focused. As you do so in a prayerful way, God will show you unique inroads into people's lives where He wants to meet the needs of their hearts.

- Character will ultimately trump giftedness, talent and the drive to achieve. So reject shortcuts that compromise your integrity or tarnish the fact that you are a follower of Jesus Christ

Three Principles for building your life

1. Own Your Own Faith

Up until this point in your Christian life, much of your spiritual experience may have been in the context of a ministry on campus or a church or group you have been a part of. In this setting, it is much like a greenhouse where the very environment is rich for growth. You have also probably been exposed to ongoing teaching and feeding from the Word, good fellowship, and effective training and equipping to reach out to others.

Now as you enter the marketplace, you potentially enter a different environment where many of the elements that you had while you were on campus will probably not be there in the quantity and quality you are used to. And in fact, you might be the most spiritually aware person in your workplace!

When you realize that you can't depend on the external influence around you to motivate you spiritually, you are at a good place for your relationship with the Lord to take on a new dimension.

This is when, as you take the primary responsibility for your growth or lack of it, you will find that you are "owning your faith" in a way that will lead you into a deeper rootedness in your trust in God as you seek Him.

Several points to keep in mind:

*   Jesus instructed us in Matthew 6:33, *"to seek first the kingdom of God."* This is so important to remember as you start your career, that you are to seek the Kingdom of God, and to trust that He will lead and empower you as He helps you establish your career.

*   *He will reward those who seek Him; "I love all who love me. Those who search for me shall surely find me."* (Proverbs 8:17, The Living Bible)

*   We really grow in our faith as we reach out to others and help them get to know God and grow in their faith.

2. Foster an Inner Life

Each one of us has an external public life, the one everyone sees, and an inner private life, that is only known to God and me. And the inner life is the one that really matters because it ultimately affects everything I do in my external life.

When people make wrong choices morally, ethically, or in relationships, it is usually because of wrong thinking in their private life. In fact, Jesus said in Mark 7:20; *"...It is the thought-life that pollutes. For from within, out of men's hearts, come evil thoughts of lust, theft, murder, adultery, wanting what belongs to others, wickedness, deceit, lewdness, envy, slander, pride, and all other folly. All these vile things come from within; they are what pollute you and make you unfit for God."* (The Living Bible)

So, the inner life needs to be cultivated and nourished, just as much as we give attention to our physical bodies by proper diet and exercise for good health. Regular, purposeful study of God's Word, personal prayer, and thoughtful reflection of what God is doing in my life, what He is saying to me, and what His perspective is on what I am going through, are the only things that will build an inner life.

The big challenge is that we live in a media driven, entertainment culture. So much so that for a person to develop a contemplative life that the scriptures speak to takes deliberate focus. We cannot text or twitter our way into a deeper relationship with God!

Jesus modeled for us the balance between a very public life and a private life where He intentionally made it a priority to get alone. There He spent time with His Father, prayed, and even wrestled through the challenges He faced.

In order to do that, it is good to have a fairly simple structure of routine in place that is very "user friendly" for you. You might already have the habit of having a regular "quiet time", but if not, here are some suggestions:

- Schedule time each week to get alone and spend time with God. Whether it is every day or several times a week, the important thing is to consistently have it as an integral part of your life which is reflected in your schedule.

- Have a Bible reading plan that is regular and systematic. Some find it helpful to follow a printed plan that guides you through a yearly reading of the Bible. There are several excellent plans that are listed at www.backtothebible.org (click on Bible Reading Guide under the Bible Studies & Devotions tab). Other people find it helpful to read three Psalms, one Proverb and one other Old or New Testament chapter every day.

- Prayer is meant to be a way of life. Not only should we be praying as we go throughout the workday, it is important to have specific times set aside to meet with God through prayer.

- Again, having a simple plan to follow can be helpful. I learned to follow the *ACTS* acronym early in my Christian life and continue to find it beneficial. It is _A_doration (which is worship), _C_onfession (which means coming before the Lord with a contrite spirit), _T_hanksgiving (expressing a heart of gratitude to the Lord), and _S_upplication (petition and intercession).

• Keeping a journal for key impressions the Lord is giving you in prayer and Bible study, as well as taking notes while listening to messages at church or at conferences, can help develop a contemplative life. It can be very helpful to review and meditate on your journal while spending time with the Lord.

3. Grow through Difficult Times

Life has its ups and downs, and adversity will come to each of us. So, it is not **if** difficult times will come, rather it is what to do **when** they occur. Sadly, for many, it is in the crucible of hardship where the weakness of their spiritual infrastructure is exposed. However, for those who have been walking with the Lord in an intimate and dynamic relationship of dependency on God, difficulty is viewed as just another step in demonstrating God's faithfulness.

But no matter where you are in your spiritual journey adversity sometimes happens. It is important to remember that you will never find yourself in a place where God has not already been. He is ready to meet you there, and He will guide and provide for you if you, seek Him with a whole heart.

Additionally, here are several key thoughts to recall in difficult times:

• Seek to balance having some key friends with whom you talk and seek spiritual and emotional support, and spending time alone with God.

• When the pressure is on and you're hurting, make it a point to move towards the Lord rather than away from Him. One of the biggest mistakes that people make in hard times is that they withdraw and shut down. Remember and follow the pattern of David in the Psalms, who for the most part of his life made it a habit of "processing his emotions" with the Lord and crying out to God when he was in pain.

- Have "anchor passages" of scripture that you refer to often that can help you get God's perspective on your life and circumstances. (i.e. Romans 8:28, Romans 8:26, Philippians 4:6-7, and other key passages God has spoken to you in the past)

- Seek to learn and grow with and in the difficult circumstance that you are in. Many try to grit their teeth and endure the situation without really growing through the experience.

- Remind yourself to look for the goodness of God. I heard a pastor say one time that, "Good and bad run on parallel tracks, and they seem to arrive at about the same time." If we are predetermined to only see the bad stuff we will miss a lot of the good things that God is doing while we are going through difficulty.

Finally, don't forget to enjoy the process of walking with God. The Apostle Paul's prayer for his friends in the Ephesian church that they would "know the love of Christ which surpasses knowledge," (Eph 3:19) and that they might "be filled up to all the fullness of God," is good to keep in focus as you continue to build your life while God empowers you to establish your career.

Questions for Discussion:

1. With which of the three traps do you most identify?

2. What are some ways that you "shine your light" in your current environment?

3. What <u>external</u> influences have you allowed to motivate your spiritual life (rather than simply a heart to know and love Christ)?

4. What have you found most helpful in developing your inner spiritual life?

Chuck Price, Campus Crusade For Christ
cprice70@earthlink.net

Chuck Price joined the staff of Campus Crusade for Christ in 1971, where he has served for 38 years. Through the years, he has been a member of the US Cabinet, Director of the Human Resource Council, and Director of the US Crisis Management team. He has also traveled and spoken in numerous countries in Asia, Europe, and North America. In 2003, Chuck served as President of Campus Crusade for Christ, Canada. He currently continues to serve with Campus Crusade in the Office of the President as Special Representative for Strategic Partnerships/Call2All as well as speaking at conferences and retreats, and mentoring and coaching various leaders around the country. In addition, he is working on a book series entitled *Getting God's Agenda, Lessons on the Journey.*. Chuck and his wife, Arlene, have been married since 1970. They have four grown children.

CHAPTER 16
Living a "Kingdom Vision"
by Mark Lewis

"And seeing the multitudes, He felt compassion for them, because they were distressed and downcast like sheep without a shepherd. Then He said to His disciples, ' The harvest is plentiful, but <u>the workers are few</u>. Therefore beseech the Lord of the harvest to <u>send out workers into His harvest</u>.' "

Matt. 9:36-38

Purposeful Transition

Life is etched with transitions. Summer gives way to fall, a driver's license expands horizons. For some, there is the painful experience of a family that was once together, fracturing apart. It is a huge adjustment going from high school to college. Some will soon move from single status to being married. Some of these changes are big, some are small. These shifts can feel like a hiccup, or a hurricane.

One of the more turbulent transitions is graduation, a change in the hurricane category. It is exciting, disorienting, and a little scary. My friend, Kent, has been sharing perspective, practical advice and hope for this transition. I want to add my encouragement. God has not lost you. He has not dimmed in His burning love for you. His purpose for you is crystal clear and brimming with possibility. (It just may not look or feel that way.) Though we get distracted, He does not. He is still all about us knowing and loving Him and helping others to know and love Him as well. He has a simple plan, and your transition is at the center of it.

Three Critical Needs

I had a good conversation a couple of weeks ago with an engineer. My new friend was three years out from being a student leader with a strong Navigator collegiate ministry. It had been a great life shaping experience. He told me what we all know, "The world of college and the world of work are so different. The transition is hard." It was evident that he continued to have a deep passion to love Christ and to have an impact for Him in the lives of others. I asked him what had helped. In his own words, he mentioned three things that I often hear. In my words, they are:

- the need for a mentor,
- like-hearted friends, and
- a kingdom vision

I am convinced that all three are indispensible. There is practical help on each of these in this book.

A Kingdom Vision

I want us to take some time on this Kingdom Vision idea because it is rare, it is fundamental, and it is often hard to keep in focus.

We are introduced to this vision at the very beginning of the Bible. In Genesis 1, God speaks creation into existence. In Genesis 2, it seems His involvement becomes more intimate. In verse 7, He forms man from the dust and face to face breathes life into him. In verse 8, you can almost imagine dirt under His fingernails as He plants a garden. In verse 15, God places the man He prepared in the garden He planted. A perfect fit. He gives Him a task with some instructions. He enters into a partnership with the man in the task.

Paul restates this beautiful plan in Ephesians 2:10, *"For we are His workmanship, created in Christ Jesus,* (The idea of a work of art, a masterpiece, uniquely hand crafted.) *for good works, which God prepared beforehand,* (Like the planted garden, God goes on ahead preparing the place and the way.) *that we should walk in them.* (He is with us as we go forward in partnership). Life and work is about taking God's creation and, in partnership with Him and others, creatively rearranging it so it is more useful, more beautiful. We can go forward in confidence that God will plant us where we can partner with Him and bring life.

Blooming Where You are Planted

In Matthew 13, Jesus shared several vignettes illustrating the answer to a question, "How does the influence of God spread into a needy world?" He shares three facets of God's plan to advance His Kingdom by using seeds as an illustration.

In verses 1-23, seeds represent <u>what</u> God uses, His Word. As we are transformed by His Word and share it with others, there are four responses. It will be brushed off by some. It will be only lightly embraced by others. Still others will start off well, but over time, they will let life smother out God's influence all together. However, as sure as grass grows in spring if we keep sowing, some will let God's truth permeate their lives.

Verses 31-32 illustrate <u>how</u> God's influence advances. Like a seed, the expansion is seemingly insignificant. It is hardly noticeable. Eventually and at times imperceptibly, but assuredly, it grows. Like a tree, it canopies <u>where it is planted</u>.

Consider verses 37-38. Along with His Word, there is something else that God uses.

Matt. 13:37-38: *"And He answered and said, "The one who sows the good seed is the Son of Man, and the field is the world; and as for the good seed, these are the sons of the kingdom;"*

In this case, who is doing the sowing? It is Jesus. Who is the seed? It is you. Think about that. I am assuming you really do want to follow our Lord's good leadership. If so, He is actively involved in placing you exactly in the "furrow" of His plan. You simply pray and go through the wisdom steps of finding a job. Does it seem rather random? Jesus' words assure us that as life's winds carry you, our great "Lord of the harvest" is actually "sowing" you. Wherever you land, you can take root and bear fruit.

So, here's the question: "What is God's plan for spreading His love into our nation and the nations of the world?" It is you partnering with God <u>in the normal course of life, living and discipling among those who do not yet know Him, wherever He plants you</u>. This is a Kingdom Vision, spreading the influence of His rule in and through the normal routine of life.

Living and Discipling

What is known as the Great Commission in Matthew 28:19-20 is not a separate activity from our normal life. The language Jesus used is "as we go", we are to "make disciples". Right where we live, work, and play, we watch for opportunities and take initiative to help others become real followers of our Lord.

A vision is a way of seeing, a perspective, and a way of looking at normal things in a different way. In John 4:35 Jesus encourages His friends to, *"Lift up your eyes, and look on the fields, that they are white for harvest."* Stop for just a minute and think. If Jesus were to sit down with you and say, "Let's take a look right where you are. Can you see your family, your friends, your workmates, your neighbors, your favorite store clerks?" Think about each one. Pray for each one. God is at work right now. Can you see any evidences of that work? Can you see yourself as "good seed", whom God has intentionally planted among them? Can you see yourself in partnership with Him in that work? Is there anyone else, any like-hearted friend with whom you can also partner?

As you are walking with God in partnership in your job or your hobby, or shopping or hanging out with family members, you are doing those activities right in the midst of a harvest field. And not just any harvest field, but the one where God planted you and is partnering with you. Like a farmer, you can patiently sow words of encouragement and prayer, love, and friendship.

"Among"

So, as you go, live and disciple <u>among</u> those who do not yet know Him. Wasn't that what Jesus did? He lived and discipled <u>among</u> us (John 1:14). Isn't that what Paul said, "You know what manner of men we proved to be <u>among</u> you." (1 Thessalonians 1:5). Isn't that the picture in Matthew 13 of yeast in flour and of a seed in the ground?

It is hard to express the importance and the power of living that word – among. He has planted you among. It is God's plan. This is why Jesus told people that the Kingdom of God was in their midst. It was because He was among them.

You are Jesus' Answer

Several years ago my family and I were living in Zimbabwe launching a Navigator ministry. We had developed a small group of Zimbabwean friends. A few had come to Christ. A few others already knew the Lord and had begun to follow Him as their best friend and leader. A few were beginning to do with others what we were doing with them. It was encouraging but small. We had been working hard, and we were tired.

During this time, I traveled to Addis Ababa, Ethiopia, to share with a similar group. I was deeply moved by the sacrifices these University students were making to follow Christ. One afternoon we went downtown to one of the largest open-air markets in Africa. I was overwhelmed by the masses of people and the pervasive poverty. I thought, "What hope do these people have? Who will help them?" I thought about our little group in Zimbabwe. We were working as hard as I knew how, but in light of these huge needs, what was the point? Was it making any difference? I laid in bed that night feeling numb.

While I was in this cloud, a friend shared two passages that have shaped me ever since. The first was Ecclesiastes 4:1-3. This book is unusual because it is written from an "under the sun" perspective. It is from the vantage point of evaluating life with natural reason, making observations about life from a ground level view. It tends toward pessimism. Almost three thousand years ago, Solomon describes a similar scene to what I had seen.

He gives a three-fold description. The people were oppressed, had no power, and no one to comfort them. His conclusion is that they would be better off dead. Pretty depressing.

Almost a thousand years later in Matthew 9:36-39, Jesus also looked on a similar scene with a similar three-fold description. They were distressed, downcast, and like sheep without a shepherd. However, His response was so different. Rather than declaring they would be better off dead, His heart went out to them. He turned to His followers and said, *"The harvest is plentiful, but the workers are few. Therefore, beseech the Lord of the harvest to send out workers into His harvest."*

My heart was encouraged. I thought, "This is what we are working on. We are not about helping our Zimbabwean friends to be 'religious' on a Sunday morning. We are helping them to live a liberated life in Christ, which gives music and light to everything they are and everything they do. And we are encouraging them to live among their friends and to make disciples in the midst of everyday life."

Someone has said that anyone can see apples on a tree, but only some can see trees in the apple. In other words, there is so much potential in each person to become healthy, vibrant, good seed which will, in turn, produce other trees. You are good seed. You can produce fruit in the lives of others you are among which, in turn, will produce more good seed. You are Jesus' answer.

Let me assure you one more time: a Kingdom vision is God's vision for you. What does our hurting world need? More than anything, it needs you as one inflamed by the love of Jesus Christ. It needs you right where God leads you next. It needs you right where you are to join others and live for Christ. As you continue – as you excel for Christ right where you are – His love comes to town and moves next door to everywhere.

Questions for Discussion:

1. What are you "intentionally" going to do to be around the lost?
2. What does it mean to "disciple" someone?
3. What does "Kingdom" mean to you?
4. What do you sense is God's "vision" for your life at this time?

Mark Lewis
marklewis@campusnavs.org

Mark Lewis has been on staff with The Navigators since 1978 and is currently the National Director for Field Integration, helping the U.S. Field ministries partner together to raise up life-long lovers and laborers for Christ, as they move from the campus to the rest of life. Mark enjoys seeing men and women know Christ and make Him known in the normal contexts of their lives. He lives in Dallas, Texas, with his wife, Janet. They have three adult children.

CHAPTER 17

THE PROTESTANT WORK ETHIC
Communicating What We Believe by How We Behave

by Mike Blackwell

It was out of the emergence of capitalism in sixteenth-century Europe that the Church's attitude toward work and the economic value system led Max Weber, the German economic sociologist, to coin a term for the new belief about work, calling it the "Protestant ethic."

It is what we today often refer to as the "Protestant work ethic." The key elements of the Protestant ethic were diligence, punctuality, deferment of gratification, and primacy of the work domain. Weber concluded that the theological beliefs that resulted in an attitude favorable to hard work and supportive of making and reinvesting profits were directly responsible for predominantly Protestant countries to be more prosperous under capitalism than those that were predominantly Catholic.

As the Puritans and Quakers began to immigrate to the New World, they packed up their belongings and their work ethic and brought it with them. They were instructed by one Puritan writer, Richard Baxter, to "Choose that employment or calling in which you may be most serviceable to God. Choose not that in which you may be most rich or honorable in the world; but that in which you may do the most good…"

They actually equated hard work with moral responsibility.

We as Christians should be aware that your greatest witness to those in the market place is how we view and conduct our daily work. If Christians at work were to conduct themselves as set forth in the manner outlined in the Bible and confirmed during the era of the Reformation, corporations and businesses would insist that their recruitment and career placement teams would be camped out at churches and Christian institutions of higher learning.

Christians should be the principled leaders and employees that are sought after for our work ethic and Christian beliefs. When you list your attributes on your resume, "Christian" should be the one that trumps your degrees and pedigrees. Having recently participated in the research of the history of Columbia International University, let me tell you about Ms. Emily Dick, a young woman from a mill village here in Columbia, South Carolina.

The cotton mill town where Emily lived was full of blue-collar families. Mill towns in the 1920's harbored all the social sins that often come with poverty stricken areas—alcoholism, domestic violence, gambling- to name a few. Across town there was a teenage girl named Emily Dick, who was a part of the Christian Endeavor Society. She taught Sunday classes for mill workers' children and recruited others to share God's love with mill worker families. Hoping to introduce them to Christ and His grace, she taught Bible, sewing, cooking, and other classes.

As the workers began to experience the saving grace of Jesus Christ, they began to change. The change was evident to H.C. Dresser, vice president of the entire mill chain. When he visited the Columbia, S.C. mill, he asked the superintendent why his mill was different - why workers in this particular mill were more dependable, more diligent and had less absenteeism. Why were there fewer fights and domestic disputes? The superintendent, a Christian, answered, "Miss Emily Dick."

When Dresser met Emily, he was so impressed, he offered her a job. The unusual job description met Emily's "calling," - teaching God's Word. According to historical documents, Mr. Dresser offered to hire Emily to start her program in all of their east coast mills. Those familiar with Columbia International University's history know that from these efforts to teach God's Word to local mill workers, Columbia Bible College was later founded.

Most historians agree John Calvin introduced the theological doctrines that, when combined with Luther's, formed a significant new attitude toward work. Calvin supported the premise that selection of an occupation and pursuing it to achieve the greatest profit possible was a religious duty.

Post Reformation Protestants also freed themselves from the "higher calling" dualism where those in "the ministry" were viewed as more "sanctified" than those who were not. Martin Luther addressed this issue head on:

"Therefore, I advise no one to enter any religious order or the priesthood; indeed, I advise everyone against it ---- unless he is forearmed with this knowledge and understands that the works of monks and priests, however holy and arduous they may be, do not differ one whit in the sight of God from the works of the rustic laborer in the field or the woman going about her household tasks, but that all works are measured before God by faith alone."

While many see the Reformation only in theological terms, others recognize it had significant impact on the social, political, and economic environment. By setting the Church free from the State and the divine rule of kings, it socially struck at society's dualistic view of work. Reformers suggested the Church was comprised of all the people of God, not just clergy. They saw all work, whether it was sacred or secular, intellectual or manual, as a way of serving God.

So, Christians in the workplace are not there by default. It is their calling. As to your work being a calling, Max Weber, German sociologist and political economist, put it this way:

"…Now it is unmistakable even in the German word *Beruf,* and still more clear in the English *calling,* a religious conception, that of a task set by God, is at least suggested."

The thing that resonated with me in this area is the intentionality. If God placed you in business, it was intentional. You are in business on purpose. God meant for you to be there. The defining word is purpose; the definitive application is that it is God's purpose and not your own. The importance, therefore, does not lie in your job per se; it lies in the purpose for which you have been called. Your work is your mission field, and the fields are ripe for harvest. (John. 4:35-38)

If we are at work, *on purpose,* can we be in the world but not of the world? First, we must be counted for Christ, not as a statistic of a morally corrupt society. We should *project* Christ into the workplace and not *reflect* what is already there ("projection" is what "should" be, whereas "reflection" represents what "is"). Given Scripture as your authority, how should we then live? The Bible is very prescriptive and tells us in Isaiah 28:17 we are to *"make justice the measuring line, and righteousness the plumb line,"* in all aspects of lives. In Ezekiel 33:10 the question is posed, *"how should we then live?"* In verse 11 we receive the answer: *"'As I live,' says the Lord."* These are not man's standards; these are God's. Christians in the work place must not lower their standards to what is expected by man. Christians must not only profess their *beliefs,* they should demonstrate it through their *behavior* as well.

So, how can you make a difference for Christ in your business and at your vocation? Simply put, as a Christian, your witness should set the standard. The Christian should be a living example of God's character and Christ's conduct. When entering the job market, one key element is "accountability." Inherent in accountability is the public profession of your faith. Unless you identify yourself with Christ, the workplace may applaud you as a moral person, but you will be measured against man's standards and not God's.

Many Christians withdraw from bearing witness to Christ because they fear the consequences of their witness. They do not make any public confession of their faith and therefore are not held accountable. Often other people's perceptions are more important to us than God's. Young Christian men and women entering the workforce should somehow "publicize" their faith in Christ.

This may best be communicated by my sharing with you a personal experience. I had been traveling and was in the office for the first time in about two weeks. Early that morning our Director of Engineering advised me that one of our new employees, Sharon, had decided to leave the company and be a "stay-at-home mom."

My initial response was, "That's great, I hope things work out well for her." But as I continued down the hall, something just didn't feel right. Sharon had been with us only three months. So I called the Director of Engineering and told him I wanted to meet with Sharon before she left.

When Sharon entered my office, I greeted her as I normally would and told her that I was sorry to hear that she was leaving. I advised her of my support for her decision. This was her last day on the job (isn't God's timing a credential of His work?).

Soon after we sat down, she began to cry uncontrollably. I said, "Sharon, are you that upset about leaving or is there something I don't know but need to?"

Her answer to me was, "Mr. Blackwell, I'm a baby Christian and the reason I'm leaving is that I have to do things on this job that I'm uncomfortable with. I really don't know if they are right or wrong, but I am not willing to take a chance, so to avoid doing something that might be wrong or not Christ-like, I'm going to leave the job."

I was shocked by her remarks. After I recovered my composure, I responded, "Sharon, I'm very sorry to hear that. Have you discussed these things with your manager?" She said she had not because she didn't know if her manager was a Christian, and she felt that if he weren't a Christian, he wouldn't understand her dilemma. She obviously wanted to do what God wanted her to do, the way God wanted her to do it.

Out of reflex, I said, "Well, Sharon, I'm a Christian. Why don't you tell me?" As she continued to cry, she raised her head and said, "I didn't know that you were a Christian, Mr. Blackwell. If I had known that, I would have come to you sooner."

Sharon and I talked for about two hours. When she left that day, I sat back in my chair, looked up at the ceiling and thought to myself, "I thought everyone in this company knew I was a Christian. I wonder why Sharon didn't know?"

It was at that moment that the Lord spoke to my heart, saying, "Look around your office! What evidence is there that you are a Christian? What is there that would have let Sharon know that you are any different from most non-Christian people?"

As I looked around my office, there was nothing on the wall that pointed to the Lord. Then I glanced over at my credenza and saw shelves of business related books, and there, sitting very unobtrusively among those books, was my relatively small Bible. I remembered placing it there, as my way of letting people know that I was a Christian. I was trying to be discreet, and apparently, I had succeeded.

We have been called to a high purpose, and your work lives are the mission field God has preordained and prepared for you.

The Hebrew word "avodah" reveals that work and worship are from the same root. It was Augustine who proclaimed "Laborare est Orare; orare est laborare…", which says "…to work is to worship; to worship is to work." In the book of Revelation we are told of four living creatures surrounding the throne of God; "they have no rest day and night, saying, Holy, holy, holy, *is* the Lord God, the Almighty, who was and who is and who is to come." The four creatures know their job description well. They are to worship and glorify God, night and day. Work is not time off from their duty to God; they simply worship while they work.

"The main end of our lives . . . is to serve God in the serving of men in the works of our callings." A person's vocation is "a certain kind of life, ordained and imposed on men by God, for the common good." William Perkins, *Treatise on the Vocations or Callings of Men.*

Questions for Discussion:

1. What are you doing so that others will know you are a "Christ Follower"?

2. Why was Luther opposed to the people becoming priests?

3. Do you believe that God has a specific career path for you? Why?

4. Should our witness be verbal as well as by modeling?

Michael Blackwell
MBlackwell@ciu.edu

Michael Blackwell worked 27 years in telecommunications, venture capital, and technology startup companies. He currently serves as Vice President for Columbia International University, where he has been since 2005. He likes to focus on ministering in the marketplace. Mike lives in Columbia, SC, with his wife, Delaine, and they have two sons and seven grandchildren.

CHAPTER 18
Life Beyond the University

by Bob Varney

What kind of job will I get? Where will I live? Will I get married? These are questions that most graduating seniors are asking. They are important questions, to be sure.

As people who know Jesus and want to follow him, we often ask for His help in answering questions like these. But does Jesus really care about my job? Or where I live? Or who accompanies me as I journey through life? Our natural answer – of course, Jesus cares; He loves me. So if He cares about my job, my location and my spouse, and if I really care about Jesus, then I ought to spend more time asking what kinds of jobs does Jesus like and why does He like them? Or, what is it about my location that matters to Him? Or, what is it about being married or not that is important to God?

1. Called to Live a Coherent Life

I remember years ago I was talking to God when I was faced with possible bankruptcy. He brought this question to my mind: "Before you started this real estate development project, why didn't you ask me about it?" As I pondered that question, I found myself surprised. I thought God only cared about the kind of person I was when I did whatever I did. Is it possible that He cared about the particular job I did? And if He did care about that, was it just because He cared about my happiness, or was there something more? Is this related to the works He had planned for me that I should walk in them?

Now that's a thought! If God has a plan for my life and that plan involves a job and a location, then I need to know more about what God cares about on this earth.

Questions are good. Curiosity is a key to learning. Keep asking questions. Keep looking to God for answers. As you do that, let's look at the larger environment in which this job, location, and idea of marriage takes place.

As a long-time business leader and now also active in the leadership of a worldwide Christian organization, I see several themes that God wants us to understand. For example, I now realize that God's design for life is coherent; that is, my life should be logically consistent across all its aspects. As you transition from the campus to the workplace, I would like to challenge you to consider new paradigms where you can see your own life as coherent without any conflicts between work and faith.

Robert Fraser reports that 3% of the Christians are called to vocational ministry[2]. That means that 97% are called to other vocations! And where do we find these other members of the Body of Christ? In the workplace, representing the domains of society where we all work such as education, business, entertainment (including arts and sports), government, and media.

There is a huge untapped potential of Christians already in the workplace. Every Christian is called by God to participate with Him as He builds His Kingdom on earth as it is in heaven. God expects Christian leaders to glorify Him through their workplace, not just while doing their work. We must all help evangelical Christianity overcome behavioral patterns that place the call of Christian workplace leaders as secondary to the call of pastors or overseas missionaries; and the role of the organizations in which they lead must also be seen as a natural and critical part of God's purpose for His kingdom on this earth at this time. Let us learn to glorify God through the workplace itself.

---

2   Robert Fraser, *Marketplace Christianity*, p.6.

2. Called to the Cities and to the Nations

The world of missions is changing, and momentum has been building for about the last decade. We now consider the workplace as a new frontier of missions. And this frontier will be moved forward largely by kingdom leaders in the workplace.

So if the workplace is important in God's eyes as an essential part of his plan, what is it supposed to look like? One answer is the expansive movement of the Spirit of God across your place of employment, your town, your city, your nation, and the world. Let's bring this down to a couple of elements that we can get our hands around. Let's look first at the city, and then in the next section, we will look at the individual.

> *The City* ... Since the city is the setting for most of our focus, how do we approach the city in the most strategic and effective manner so that we are seeing the possibility for everyone to know someone who truly follows Jesus? For this element, we look at the peace and well-being of the city itself. We have to understand on the macro-level what the key associations are of those who live or work in the city and find ways to be "insiders" in those avenues of association.

These two elements of the city and the individual are not new. However, what is new is the call to see movements of God's Spirit everywhere, which requires us to approach old objectives in new ways. Our spiritual development process cannot focus on curricula of how-to's, but on new paradigms and problem-solving. Our ministry goals can't be contained merely in "reaching" lost individuals out of the world but must be more strongly focused on "launching" true followers **into** the world. Further, we must recognize that the Body of Christ is already engaged in most global cities. No matter what our "Christian affiliation", we must work alongside one another, bringing our unique gifts to the table and ensuring that we are seated together, on equal terms, as we work together for the city. We cannot afford only to seek to be the best Jesus followers **in** a place; we must seek to be the best **for** that place.

We realize that within each country, there are one or more mega-cities. In fact, in most countries, the population of the mega-cities may be substantially the population of the entire nation. If we do not effectively penetrate the workplace in these cities, it means we don't attain the mission to which God has called us.

We believe that movements will happen everywhere as people from within the places where they currently spend their time spread God's kingdom through the people they currently influence. Increasingly, peoples' natural point of intersection with others is their workplace. While not their only intersection, the workplace, more than the home or the local church, is increasingly shaping the values, culture, and accessibility of the individual.

It would be insufficient to view the city simply through the lens of one's own denomination or the presence of a group of "vocational Christians." Instead, we must look at the whole city, *considering* its spiritual and physical needs on personal and corporate levels. Emphasis must be given to the word "consider" here. We are asking for a shift in our vantage point. It's easy to assume that by mentioning the "whole city", that we are suggesting that one's own efforts *do* the whole city's work. By no means! Reality is that there are many believers already engaged in cities, and we are one in Spirit and Faith with them.

3. Called to Mobilize, Equip, and Release Individuals for His Kingdom

There is a great need in societies around the world for a better life. As followers of Jesus, we are commanded to pray for God's will on earth as it is in heaven, and we know that the expansion of God's Kingdom on this earth would actually be very beneficial to all peoples.

> *The Individual...* How do we see a force of individual movement launchers mobilized and multiplying in cities in a way that societies are improved, and everyone knows someone who truly follows Jesus?

This front addresses the individuals who, as true followers of Jesus, are part of the movement of expanding the kingdom through their spheres of influence. We need to see this band of movement launchers grow in number and in personal depth as Christian leaders to the extent that movements everywhere are a real possibility through them.

For workplace individuals, who will be mobilized as movement catalysts in their workplace, what picture do we expect to see?

We expect to see these individuals:

- Living a vibrant life through a deep relationship with Christ

- Sowing seeds of Christ's message *all the time*

- Doing the right thing where all decisions are based on God's righteousness

- Realizing that their daily activities have kingdom impact and instructional value for current and future followers-of-Christ *(seeing "discipleship" through a different lens)*

- Re-aligning their world-view and outlook toward Kingdom values all the time

- Harvesting new believers as God moves in their lives

- Behaving with an acute awareness of the value of multiplying one's whole self and desiring to get into apprenticeship relationships

Each true follower's example will help others experience a new life in Christ every day in everything, especially in the workplace, including life-changing discipleship, connecting the lost to Christ, and instilling in others the sense of need and confidence necessary to pass-on God's movement mission.

The basic needs of these Christians haven't changed in terms of the DNA that makes them multiplying disciples. However, the manner and context of learning and transformation are radically different, in fact unique to each city and domain.

Let's step back and look at what God might see as he looks at a city. It is as though we were trapped in a great water tower above our city with only a very small pipe to get the message of our lives to the others in the city. We need to find ways to release the power of the potential kingdom leaders that God has chosen already.

Because they do not yet know Him, some leaders will need to be introduced to Jesus Christ. There are other leaders who are already true followers of Jesus and working hard in their role in God's kingdom on this earth. However, most potential kingdom leaders do not even know they are and do not know how to reflect God, replenish the earth, and reproduce. We need to find ways to mobilize these kingdom leaders, which means we must (1) awaken them to the condition of their workplace and surrounding society; (2) help them discover their role in leading life-change in those places; (3) equip them with tools and methodologies as well as always refreshing the basics of Christian living; and (4) release them right back where they are working as effective, reproducing laborers in God's kingdom.

As these kingdom leaders are mobilized, the picture we see is a large number of pipes carrying the water of life into our cities and all over the societies of the world.

There is virtually no limit to the style, shape, or placement of movements led by these kingdom leaders. Some work in a specific domain, whereas some have put networks together for all domains. Some bring people together with events or training; others find leaders by relationships. Some operate a business; some operate as ministries; and still others operate as non-profits providing services for fees. Some work with local governments; some work with businesses; some work with other ministries. Some measure results as decisions for Christ; some measure results by the outcomes of lives lived for Christ.

It is evident that the influence of such efforts does not stop at the boundary of personal transformation in Christ. Individual transformation must be expanded to societal transformation as well. This is informative for us as we seek to actively engage the culture in every aspect -- spiritually, socially, and economically -- on both an individual and corporate level. We can also look forward to a vibrant life in God's kingdom while enjoying the peace of a coherent life without internal conflicts.

Conclusion

Let us now get back to our questions – what job, what location, and who travels with me on this journey of life? Knowing that my college environment will be no more, and I will find myself in the 40-50-hour-a-week workplace, how can I get prepared? Who can go with me?

Be intentional about the pursuit of each of these three questions. Pray about them with a small group of friends. Study them together. And especially seek what God says about His mission on this earth. For example, consider what God means when he says:

1. *"Thy will be done on earth as it is in heaven."* (Matthew 6:10)

2. *"God was reconciling the world to himself."* (2 Corinthians 5:19)

3. *"Be fruitful and multiply and replenish the earth".* (Genesis 1:28)

4. *"I will make you into a great nation...and all peoples on earth will be blessed through you."* (Genesis 12:2-3)

5. *"Build houses and live in them...seek the welfare of the city...for in its welfare you will find welfare."* (Jeremiah 29:5-7)

6. *"Pray earnestly to the Lord of the harvest to send out laborers into his harvest."* (Luke 10:2)

7. *"Teach them all that I have commanded you."* (Matthew 28:20)

Questions for Discussion:

1. Why is the "city" important to God?

2. Why is God more interested in individuals, cities, and nations than in organizations and institutions? Give examples.

3. What does it mean to have a "Kingdom" viewpoint?

4. What can you do to have an "intentional" impact in your workplace?

Bob Varney
bob.varney@ccci.org

Bob Varney was an entrepreneur for 25 years, leading a number of high-tech companies. For the last decade, he has been senior advisor to the president of Campus Crusade for Christ. Bob holds a PhD in computer science. He lives with his wife of 43 years in McLean, VA, and they have two married daughters and three grandsons.

APPENDIX I

How to Know the Will of God for Your Life

A few things that God has taught me over the years are:

1. It is much more important that we get to <u>know Him</u> than worrying about what His specific will is for this time in our life. As we know Him intimately, then He allows us to see what He wants us to become and to do. "Being" is more important than "doing".

2. It is very important that we are <u>willing to surrender</u> to do His will when He has shown us what we are to do. This is not an option that we are free to reject. Once the Holy Spirit reveals God's will to us, then we need to immediately do it. It is really summed up by "TRUST and OBEY".

3. The major life events over the sixty plus years of my life have been determined by <u>three</u> things: the providence of God, divine appointments, and my choices (good and bad ones). The more that we relax and just walk with Him and trust Him, the easier it is for us to see His leading.

I. Preparation for Knowing God's Will

a. Realize God is more interested in us knowing His will than we are in knowing it or doing it. (Ephesians 5:17)

b. He Promises us His guidance. (Psalm 32:8)

c. He will judge us for what we do. (2 Corinthians 5:10)

d. It simplifies our life…Christ's *only* aim was to please God. (John 6:38)

e. It is best…(Romans 12:2)…good, acceptable, perfect. (Deuteronomy 5:29, Colossians 1:9,10)

f. God's will sometimes is general, applying to all of us.

g. God has at other times a *specific* purpose and plan for each of our lives.

II. Principles of Knowing God's Will

a. Are you committed to Christ? (Romans 12:1)

b. Are you committed to doing God's will? (John 7:17, Luke 9:23)

c. Are you "confessed up" of any known sin? (Psalm 66:18, I John 1:9)

d. Are you obedient to what God has already shown you? (Psalm 119:59, 60)

e. Are you in daily fellowship with God through His Word and prayer? (Psalm 5:3)

f. Are you in "neutral," willing for the matter to fall either way? Ask God to reveal whether you are in neutral. If not, continue to pray that God's desires will be your desires.

g. What do you want to do? God will either give you your desires or change your desires to something better. (Psalm 37:4,5)

h. Are you aware that Biblically, God's perspective of our situation is usually far different from ours? (Psalm 103:19)

III. Procedure for Discovering God's Will:

a. Get the facts. (Proverbs. 24:3,4; see Living Bible)

b. God's Word (Ps. 119:105)

c. Godly counsel (Proverbs 15:22; 24:6)

   d. God-given gifts (Romans 12; I Corinthians 12; Ephesians 4)

   e. Providential circumstances (Luke 1:52; Psalm 4:8)

   f. Prayer (John 16:24)

   g. Prompting of the Holy Spirit (John 16:13)

   h. Peace (John 14:27)

IV. Pressing on to do God's will

   a. By *faith*, step out and *do* what God has directed.

   b. FAITH + ACTION = RESULTS

   c. Timing is also important.

V. Pitfalls to Avoid

   a. Don't trust conscience only.

   b. Don't worry about His will for all of your entire future. Take one step at a time!

   c. Viewing apparent acts of disobedience in our lives or others resulting in good results.

   d. Viewing apparent acts of obedience resulting in bad results.

   e. Letting another person (parent, friend, counselor) decide for you.

   f. Thinking that God cares only about your major decisions.

VI. How Priorities Help Determine God's Will in a Certain Area

- This is a system that I have used:

   1. List your priorities *in order.*

   2. If you have a decision that benefits the *top* priorities and breaks

even or even hurts the bottom ones, it may be okay. The key is to keep your <u>top priorities</u> in mind when considering what God is asking you to do.

My list:

1. Personal relationship to God - (Matthew 6:33)

2. Mate - (I Peter 3:7; Ecclesiastes 9:9)

3. Family - (Deuteronomy 6:6,7)

4. Job - (Proverbs 12:22)

5. Friendships - (Ecclesiastes 4:9,10)

6. Health - (I Corinthians 6:19)

7. Ministry to others - (II Corinthians 5:17,18; Philemon 1:7)

8. Location of where we will live

9. Church life or Christian organization or ministry

10. Personal Preference

11. Money - (Proverbs 10:16, see Living Bible)

12. Leisure Time

Valid Principles on Conduct:

1. Does the Bible say it is wrong? (John 14:21)

2. Will it hurt my body? (I Corinthians 6:19)

3. Will it hurt my mind? (Philippians 1:2-5)

4. Will it enslave me? (I Corinthians 6:12)

5. Is it good stewardship in time, talent, etc? (I Corinthians 4:2)

6. Will it glorify God? (Romans 14:21; I Corinthians 10:31)

7. Will it profit and edify others? (I Corinthians 10:23,33)

8. Will it help me to serve or will it be a stumbling block to others and hurt my testimony? (I Corinthians 9:19; I Corinthians 8:9) Proverbs 14:21)

9. Is it worth imitating, or would I rather keep it a secret? (I Corinthians 11:1; Philippians 4:19)

10. Does it have an appearance of evil? (Romans 13:12,13)

11. Is it the best for me to be involved in? (Psalm 25:12-14, See Living Bible) (Philippians 1:9, 10)

12. Is it of benefit to me (spiritually, physically, emotionally, mentally, and socially)?

13. Will it be a thorn causing anxious cares, desire for riches, or desire for pleasure? (Mark 4:19; Luke 8:14)

14. Is it a weight - (neither good nor bad but slows us down)? (Hebrews 12:1,2)

15. Am I willing to wait? (Psalm 37:34)

HOMEWORK:

1. List these *priorities* in the proper order for your life: (Number 1 through 14)

Location (Where you live)	Personal Relationship to God
Leisure Time	Church Life
Health	Personal Preference
Mate	Ministry to Others
Job Fulfillment	Family
Money	Friendships
Friendship	Family (Kids)

2. What is *one* decision you need to determine God's will about right now? (Pray about it daily.)

3. What is *one* major decision which you made this year which was in God's will? Give benefits.

4. What *biblical passages* did you use for guidance in this area?

5. What *people* do you go to for counsel in major decisions?

6. Name *one* Bible character that made a major decision (in recent Bible reading).

Right Decision ⟳ Benefits

Wrong Decision ⟳ Results

APPENDIX II

Web Sites for Your Transition and Resources for Small Groups

FLUX
www.intervarsity.org/alumni/resource

Baptist Collegiate Ministry (BSU)
www.oubsu.org/resources/resources.php

Campus Crusade for Christ
www.campuscrusade.com/group_studies.htm

Campus Renewal Ministries
www.campusrenewal.org

Christian Challenge
www.unlchallenge.com

Christianity Today
www.christianitytoday.com/biblestudies/

Church Teams
www.churchteams.com/ct/

College Seniors and Recent Grads
www.WorkplaceRevolutions.com

Discipleship Library
www.discipleshiplibrary.com/index/php

Inside Work
www.insidework.net

Intervarsity Press
www.ivpress.com/cgi-ivpress/uber_subject.pl/uber_id=8

Navigators
www.b2g.org

NavPress
www.navpress.com/landing/biblestudies.aspx

Student Mobilization
www.stumo.org

Urbana (Intervarsity)
www.urbana.org/bible-studies

Worldview Matters
www.worldviewmatters.com

APPENDIX III

Recommended Workplace Ministries / Web Sites

Lifestyle Impact Ministries (Kent and Davidene Humphreys)
www.lifestyleimpact.com

Fellowship of Companies for Christ Int. (FCCI / Christ@Work)**
www.fcci.org

Biblical Worldview
www.worldviewmatters.com
www.biblicalworldviewmatters.blogspot.com

Biblical Worldview
www.BiblicalWorldviewTraining.org

Blackaby Ministries
www.blackaby.org/marketplace

Business as Mission Network
www.businessasmissionnetwork.com

Business by the Book (Crown Financial Ministries)
www.crown.org/Tools/

Business Proverbs
www.businessproverbs.com

C -12 Group**
www.C12group.com

CBMC (USA)
www.cbmc.com

Christianity 9 to 5 (Professor Michael Zigarelli)
www.epiphanyresources.com/9to5/

Christians in Commerce
www.christiansincommerce.org

Convene (formerly BBL Forum) **
www.convenenow.com

Corporate Chaplains of America
www.chaplain.org

Crossroads Career Network
www.crossroadscareer.org/

Crosswalk.Com
www.crosswalk.com/careers/

Executive Ministries
www.execmin.org

Faith and Work Resources
www.faithandworkresources.com

Full Gospel Business Men's Fellowship
www.fgbmfi.org

Inside Work
www.insidework.net

Integrity Resource Center
www.integritymoments.com

International Coalition of Workplace Ministries
www.icwm.net

International Christian Chamber of Commerce
www.iccc.net

Intervarsity-Urbana-Whole Life Stewardship
www.urbana.org/whole-life-stewardship

Lausanne Business as Mission
http://www.lausanne.org/documents/2004forum/LOP40_IG11.pdf

Marketplace Chaplains USA
www.mchapusa.com

Marketplace Leaders
www.marketplaceleaders.org

Marketplace Network
www.marketplace-network.net

MEDA
http://www.meda.org/WhoWeAre

Mike McLoughlin
blog.mike.mcloughlin.com/

Priority Associates (Campus Crusade)
www.priorityassociates.org

Scruples (YWAM)
www.scruples.net/

Selling Among Wolves Sales Seminar
www.sellingamongwolves.net

Strategic Christian Services
www.gostrategic.org

Wise Counsel**
www.askwisecounsel.com/

Worklife (formerly His Church at Work)
www.worklife.org

Workplace Ministry Training
www.WorkplaceMinistryTraining.com

Avodah Institute
http://www.avodahinstitute.com (under construction)

**These organizations primarily serve CEO's and business owners through small groups that meet weekly or monthly.

APPENDIX IV

Resources for Evangelism and Discipleship

The Compass - **A tool to help new followers of Christ by Lanphier Press**
www.lanphierpress.com/Compass.htm

Operation Timothy - Discipleship tool by CBMC
www.cbmc.com/store/product/114/40

Discipleship studies and tools – Navigators and NavPress
www.navpress.com/landing/discipleship.aspx

Steps to Peace with God by Billy Graham
www.billygraham.org/SH_StepstoPeace.asp

The Bridge to Life
www.navigators.org/us/resources/illustrations/items

The Four Spiritual Laws by Campus Crusade
www.campuscrusade.com/Tracts_and_Booklets

Wheaton College
www.wheaton.edu/BusEcon/

APPENDIX V

Questions on Your Transition

These are questions from those who are currently in transition from the campus to the workplace:

God's Will

There are so many seemingly good options and opportunities; how can I know which one is God's will for me? (See Appendix 1)

How do I know what I am supposed to "do with my life", particularly in this time of transition?

How do I differentiate between my plan and God's plan?

How do I bring together my many desires and the open doors?

How do I learn to wait while God is turning my heart and opening my eyes to the next step, and how do I know when it is the right time to transition?

Career

How much of a role should my feelings and the passions of my heart play in making a career decision?

How do I distinguish between my thoughts and desires and what God is calling me to do?

How do I know which career to go into when I do not feel a particular calling?

What does it look like to trust God with my career choice?

Should I look for a career or just take the next step as God reveals it?

Community

How do I find, get plugged into, and cultivate community in a new place where I do not know anyone?

How do I find a new support system and an uplifting group when I know few believers?

What does it look like to invest into a new community while still trying to maintain relationships from the previous one in which I invested so much?

Local Church

How do I start looking for the right local church, and how do I adapt?

Do I have to compromise if the churches do not look like my college church?

Since I was only in a college ministry, how to I transition into an "established" church?

Workplace

What are some of the ways that I can integrate my faith and bring Jesus into a secular workplace?

How do I transition from the flexibility of college life to the structure of the 9 to 5 corporate workplace?

How do I stay strong and faithful when I am surrounded by a culture of unbelievers who prioritize everything else above faith?

How can I make a difference for God's kingdom when moving from an environment of strong Christians into the real world?

How do I transition from having a boss who is like minded in Christ to one who may not be, and how can I submit to an authority whom I do not respect?

How do I deal with others' (parents' generation) "expectations" for my life when my view of success is so much different than theirs?

Ministry

What are some types of ministries that I should get involved in once I graduate and enter the workplace?

As I am stepping down from a leadership position in a student ministry, how to I continue to be involved in the "real world" away from college?

How can I find the ministry where I can be the most effective?

APPENDIX 6

A Message to Campus Ministry Staff

Thank you for giving your life to prepare our next generation of Christian leaders. Davidene and I have supported through our prayers, finances, and encouragement a number of campus ministries like yours during the last thirty years. I really appreciate your sacrifice to raise your own financial support in most cases, to serve these students for a few brief years, and then to send them out into the world to serve Christ. We were both student leaders in a campus ministry while in school. I hope that this frank discussion will be a help to you as you dialogue about these critical transition issues with your organizational leadership, your graduates, your donors, and the students who are currently in your ministry. I do know that a number of ministries have been working on this transition problem for years, but there has been little interaction with workplace ministries. Most of the work has been between the divisions of large ministries. So, even though I have very limited understanding of campus ministries and the tremendous challenges that you face with limited funds and staff, my heart tells me that we must address this issue of transition. We must conserve more of the fruit of your efforts and what the Holy Spirit has done in the lives of these students. I think that those of us who are employed in the marketplace, and leaders in workplace ministries, missions, local churches, and educational institutions in the Body of Christ need to dialogue more with you who are leading student ministries. We must begin to build effective bridges to assist in the transition for these students into their next stage of their lives.

For many years I have had the privilege of speaking on campuses for a number of student ministries. I have also spoken in the business schools of a number of universities both in the undergraduate and graduate programs. Then, I have been able to relate to the graduates as they moved into the workplace. For a long time, I have seen the need for bridges to be built between the campus and the workplace. I did not know which audience I should address in this book. I asked myself if I should address the ministry staff in the field on the campuses, or the leaders of the organizations, or their donors, or the students themselves? God finally led me to write primarily to the graduating students (the "masses" and not necessarily your "core" team) and to those who have just joined the workforce. However, the other groups may also find these thoughts to be helpful. This book simply becomes another tool in your toolbox that you can use in your campus ministry to prepare the graduates as they leave the campus.

Target Groups:

1. **80%** - Are those students in your ministry who have not spent the most time with you and the staff. These thoughts will complement what you have given them and emphasize the teaching that they did not receive because they were not in the CORE of your ministry. Your student leaders, and the ones who have been most active in your ministry (the 20%), have been trained by you in most of these principles, and most of them will be mature enough to adapt to their new surroundings. Those leaders will be encouraged by these thoughts, but they are not the target audience. Those student leaders will be able to use this booklet as a tool as they encourage fellow grads who are leaving the campus with them or that they meet as they enter the workplace full time.

2. **Those on the Fringe** - Many students have attended your events but have never really been involved on a regular basis in your ministry. These comments will be very helpful to them because they have not been exposed to years of training. This is something that you can share with them as they leave the campus.

3. **The Drop Outs** - They attended your events in their freshman year or were involved for a short time, but then dropped out. You and your key students can share this tool with them as they leave the campus.

If they still are being convicted by the Holy Spirit, this gives you one more opportunity to have an investment into their lives.

4. **Those Who Were Never Involved** - They came to the campus after being active during their high school years in their church youth group. But, because of getting off track, class schedules, or working schedules, they never got active in a student ministry or activity.

Issues:

1. **Calling** - Only 10% or less of the students in a university ministry go into "vocational" Christian ministry. (The percentage would be higher of those graduating from a Christian college.) This ministry might be to a student campus ministry, pastoral staff or church ministry, church planting, overseas missions, or others. That leaves 90% of the graduates that will go into the "secular workplace". Many of those who have the greatest heart for God struggle with guilt in making a choice between their gifts, talents, and passion, versus the "call" to go into "full-time vocational service". So, they begin their careers feeling like "second-class citizens" in the Kingdom of God. Those of us in leadership must be careful to emphasize that every graduate is "called" into the full-time ministry of reconciliation, even though they will be paid by employers in the secular workplace.

2. **Drifting** - When graduates move to another city and get a job, they seldom find a church or ministry that looks and feels like the campus ministry that they just left. Many of them drift around, attending church occasionally, even though just a few years before they may have been active in campus ministries.

3. **Coming Home** - Most of these students eventually get married, have children, and only then find their way back into the organized church. Many come back because they want to share their Christian values with their young children. But, this may be five to seven years later, and the flame that once burned brightly in their hearts has been nearly put out.

4. **Pathway** - There is no pathway that is clearly marked out for grads who do NOT go into the professional vocational ministry to transition into a local church that will minister to them and through them in their new workplace situation.

5. **Adjusting** - Many of these young adults struggle with adjustments to marriage, a stressful job, finances, or raising children. So, their spiritual life, that was such a high priority in college, gets put on the back burner and ignored. This often leads to guilt, but little change.

6. **Lost Fruit** - Therefore, as the Body of Christ, we lose much of the fruit of campus ministries. Yes, there are the large numbers of new converts and some good discipleship that is taking place. However, much of that fruit is lost in the transition. If this were a "for profit" business, the investors would ask for changes to be made so that the ROI (Return on Investment) could be increased. As a donor to student ministries, a leader in the Body of Christ, a former leader of a workplace organization, and a business leader who wants a good return on my investment, I want to see the fruit of your ministry preserved. I want to see bridges built between student ministries, churches, and workplace ministries so that these transitions can be smoother as we focus together on preserving the fruit of your labors.

Causes:

1. **Dualism** - The number one cause of this situation is that we have a "dualistic" thinking, which divides the sacred and the spiritual. This unbiblical philosophy has impacted much of our strategic thinking at every level of ministry. This is not only true in many student ministries, but it is also representative of many local churches. I found it even to be permeating the church in China! We must clearly understand the "priesthood of every believer" and the responsibility of every believer to be a full-time ambassador for Christ. For more on this topic, please obtain David Dawson's *"The Priesthood of Every*

Believer, Resolving the Clergy / Laity Distinction," or my book, *"Christ@ Work Opening Doors, Impacting Your Workplace for Jesus Christ."*

2. **Emphasis** - As staff on a campus ministry, you would tell me that you want to equip ALL of the students for their next stage of life and career. You would disagree with the assumption that many ministries only emphasize the "real spiritual positions" of missionary, pastor, and campus ministry. However, the student in many ministries quickly understands that, if he or she is a true follower of Christ, they should go to seminary or directly into full-time student ministry. These student leaders that are headed to vocational ministry are highlighted on the platform, on the leadership team, and in the summer programs. Some student ministries put tremendous pressure on these students to redeem this time for spiritual training. Some are discouraged from pursuing "secular" pursuits like summer internship programs or getting a job to make money to help pay for education expenses.

3. **Measurements** - There are thousands of good campus ministries that are doing great work around the world. Campus Crusade, Inter Varsity, the Navigators, Christian Challenge, and hundreds of other large ministries have impacted millions of students for Christ over the last few generations. Many local churches and denominations have various levels of campus ministries. These ministries and their staffs are focused on a <u>few measurable goals.</u> (Your organizational leadership and we as business leaders, donors, and board members have demanded these goals from you.) How many students come to Christ? How many students are discipled? How many students go on summer mission programs? How many go to key student conferences? How many go on staff and in many cases raise their own support? We become focused on expanding and growing the ministry rather than equipping ALL graduates to be effective AFTER they leave the campus. Unfortunately, we often are just focused on the "silo" of the campus ministry and not the workplace in which most of them will be serving. So, the students are equipped with some tools and situations which do not fit in the cities and the workplaces to which they move.

4. **Organizational Support** - The level of support of the individual staff and the campus team from ministry executives, boards, and donors in many cases is directly reflected by how "successful they are in reaching the above "measurable" goals. Perhaps in some cases. we have adopted "secular measurements" to hold you accountable for Kingdom objectives.

5. **Donor Support** - The primary focus of the campus ministry that is presented to donors is on how the staff continues to grow the ministry on each campus. How many campuses are we on? How many countries are we in? The key number is new staff and the increasing budget. These are the key results that your ministry shares with donors and their supporters. The irony is that the better job that student ministries do in equipping graduates to do well in the workplace, the easier it will be for them to raise support from them as donors in the future. But, are student ministries preparing the graduates to minister in their workplaces? Or are they content to prepare them to become active in local "church" activities and support the campus ministries that trained them? In many cases, the student ministry may become a competitor for funds of the local church or vice versa.

6. **Professional / Laity Divide** - While the focus shifts many times to the 10% of the students, and not the 90% that goes into the workplace, student ministries want the 90% graduating into the workplace to fund the ministry of their peers, who joined the staff of the ministry. This reaffirms the dualism and class system. "If you cannot GO, then you can pray and give." We miss the huge opportunity in front of us to equip them to represent Christ right where they are in the secular workplace with the training that they received on the campus.

7. **Moving On** - Most graduates will move out of the area after graduation. Many key universities are not in huge metropolitan areas. So, in most cases, the graduates end up in another city and state. If students get a job in the local area and try to stay connected, it makes

them feel better. However, this only delays the adjustment that they will have to make when they finally make the break and learn to cope in the next phase of life.

8. **Mentoring Connections** - Many campus ministries and Christian colleges do try to connect with their graduates, but the objective is normally to raise funds. There are a very few ministries that are trying to establish mentoring programs to link seniors and grad students with leaders in the local community or surrounding communities. However, there are far too few of these programs, and most are under-developed and under-emphasized.

Solutions:

1. **Priesthood of Believers** - We must look at all of our language and procedures and take the "secular / sacred divide" out! Emphasize the priesthood of ALL believers and the calling of each to represent Christ. Ministry is NOT an activity but is all of life. Professionals are to assist the Body of Christ in equipping, training, leading, and other responsibilities, but they are to equip ALL to do the work of the ministry. Each of us is to have a vibrant relationship with the risen Christ.

2. **Full-Time Ambassadors** - We should change all the disciples' emphasis in the earliest programs to their message: God wants ALL of us to be full-time ambassadors for Him. Emphasize that every calling is a divine one and a "full-time" responsibility. Share stories not only of those who go on staff or into missions, but of those who are serving as leaders in the community in education, government, the marketplace, the media, the sports and entertainment world, the family, and vocational ministry. Have more alumni who are in the workplace speaking to student groups. Be very careful not to have a majority of ministry "professionals" of staff and pastors speaking on your platform to your students. Remember, it is NOT what you say that is the most important, but who are the MODELS that you present?

3. **Internships** - Encourage not only summer missions but internships in companies owned and led by strong followers of Christ, and have your students work for large secular corporate companies. Then, they can come back to the campus and share challenges and experiences. Constantly bring back former grads, who are not only successful in their career, but also are mature believers.

4. **Mentoring** - Establish formal mentoring programs during the senior year with key Christian leaders in the community. Many in their 50's and 60's would love to make an investment into a future leader. Mentoring programs may be our greatest opportunity to build these bridges of long-term relationships.

5. **Partnerships** - Begin partnerships with both local churches and churches in key metropolitan areas which are closest to your campus. Develop these relationships as key alliance partners. Point to models of local bodies of believers that most closely represent your philosophy of ministry. If there are not any good ones close by in those cities, then start one.

6. **Models** - Expose the students to various forms of churches, house churches, cell groups, and other forms of the Body. Show them models that will work with their generation. Expose them to a number of workplace ministries that they can plug into as they move into their new city and environment. Spend some real effort in building bridges to help them make a smooth transition as possible.

Conclusion:

I welcome your comments and suggestions. This is NOT my area of expertise. I just see the results of student ministries as the graduates come into the workplace. We need more of them to be engaged sooner in effective ministry in order to not lose years of opportunities to minister. May God give you and your organizations new effective ways to partner with others in order to build bridges of transition that will help your graduates to be more effective for Christ and His Kingdom. I know that together we can help the Body of Christ to bring more glory to Him in all the communities into which your graduates are being sovereignly sent by Him.

Bulk Quantities-

We want this book to be easily acquired by your ministry to be given away in large quantities. It is available for your student ministry at inexpensive bulk prices for you. You may contact us through our web site at www.lifestyleimpact.com or with the information at the back of this book. Once some of your workplace leader donors see the subject matter, they will gladly write a check for you to buy several boxes for your many student contacts.

Other Books by Kent and Davidene Humphreys

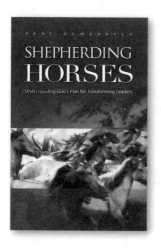

Shepherding Horses (Volume I)

Understanding God's Plan for Transforming Leaders

Lifestyle Impact Publishing

Kent's most well-received book yet! This 50-page guide to Understanding God's Plan for Transforming Leaders is a must-read for any pastor and the strong and driven business leaders (horses) that he shepherds. Kent looks at a biblical view of "horses" and shares with pastors an effective way to partner with these business leaders – building bridges of acceptance and understanding.

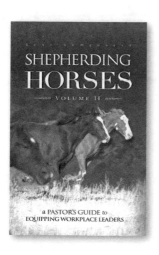

Shepherding Horses (Volume II)

A Pastor's Guide for Equipping Workplace Leaders

Lifestyle Impact Publishing

In this book, Kent encourages pastors to invest in the incredible resource they have – the business leaders in their churches. The book is full of practical and possible ideas for shepherding, encouraging and releasing these leaders for ministry in the place they understand best - their business world.

Housekeeping Skills for Kids

Teaching Them Doesn't Have to Be a Chore

Lifestyle Impact Publishing

Davidene's book, "Housekeeping Skills for Kids: Teaching Them Doesn't Have to be a Chore", has proven to be a best-seller. In it she provides simple and practical steps for parents of any-aged children to train them in skills that they will need to create and run their own home someday. Full of stories, encouragement, and ideas, this book is an inspiration to any parent trying to develop their kids' domestic skills. It covers everything from cooking, to organization, to use of tools, to planning great parties.

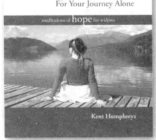

Encouragement for Your Journey Alone

Meditations of Hope for Widows

Tate Publishing

This wonderful little book is a gift of hope and encouragement for widows. It is a compilation of meditations, which the author suggests reading at the pace of one per week. This gives thinking and praying time over each meditation. Kent Humphreys has written a letter each month for nine years to many widows; this book has been birthed from that long-standing ministry and is a special gift to women who have a special place in God's heart.

KENT HUMPHREYS has been a business leader for over forty years. While owning and operating a nationwide general merchandise distribution business, he worked with the nation's largest retailers. Since selling the family business in 1997, Kent continues to be involved in real estate, private equities, and a medical distribution business. From 2002 through 2007, he was president of *Fellowship of Companies for Christ, International,* an organization that equips and encourages Christian business owners who desire to use their companies as a platform for ministry. Kent now serves as a worldwide ambassador for FCCI (Christ@Work).

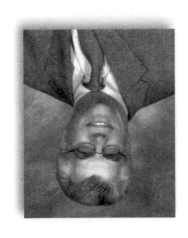

For many years, Kent has spent much of his time ministering to business leaders, pastors, and students across the country through speaking, writing, and mentoring. He has spoken in seminaries across the United States and overseas and at numerous international conferences. He travels extensively overseas several times each year. He served for many years on the boards of directors of The Navigators, Integris Hospital, seminaries, and other charitable organizations. *Christ@Work In Your Transition from the Campus to the Workplace* is the sixth book that Davidene and Kent have worked on together. Kent and Davidene have three children and eight grandchildren, and make their home in Oklahoma City.

The Gracious Woman
Retaineth Honor...

Personal Bible Studies for the Christian Woman

Lifestyle Impact Publishing

The Gracious Woman, which was originally written by Memie Stuart, has been revised and re-published by Davidene Humphreys, Memie's daughter. It is comprised of 24 lessons, including such subjects as "The Christian Woman and her relationship to God, to her husband, to her children, and to her community." A complete teacher's guide is available, so this is an ideal course of study for an individual or a group.

Christ@Work – Opening Doors

Impacting Your Workplace for Jesus Christ

Lifestyle Impact Publishing

Kent shares how you can impact your co-workers, vendors, customers, and even your competitors for Jesus Christ in your workplace. He shows you what to do, how to do it, and when to start. He shares the steps to walking through open doors in the workplace that God will undoubtedly provide for you.

Between the Phone Call and the Funeral

Tate Publishing

Have you ever wondered what to do for a grieving family? Do you find yourself taking food to the house, feeling a bit nervous about what to say? Do you end your visit by saying something like, "If you need anything, call me"? You mean it, but you are not sure what would be helpful. This book is your answer. It is the best gift you could give, and the ideas in it are the best things you could do for these hurting friends. Buy one now, and have it before you need it, because you will need it. Buy another one to put in your church's office for the next church family who needs it. Helping those who grieve is a wonderful ministry, one which blesses the giver as much as the receiver.

Show and then Tell

*Presenting the Gospel Through
Daily Encounters*

Moody Publishing

How can we become confident in sharing our faith, both in action and word? How do we make ourselves available to others, Christian and non-Christian, to share what God has done in our own lives? How do we encourage them to trust God more? In "Show and then Tell", Kent and Davidene encourage Christians that God has called every one of us to evangelism. He has given us unique personalities and gifts to reach our world for Christ. Our lives have extraordinary possibilities when we call on Jesus to give us the strength to share our faith — naturally.